Start Your Internet Business: 36 Things You Need to Know Now

Edited by:
Dr. Christina McCale
Dr. Richard D. Moody

Featuring:
Dennis Becker
Willie Crawford
Nicole Dean
Reed Floren
Connie Ragen Green
Jane Mark
Susanne Myers
Rachel Rofe
Marlon Sanders
Tahir Shah
Dr. Mani Sivasubramanian

CONTENTS

ACKNOWLEDGEMENTS

A research and book production such as this comes together, thanks to the talents of a great number of people. We would like to acknowledge those who helped make this project possible - in hopes that the readers of this book may have an easier process in starting their business.

Willie Crawford, our business partner and expert author in this series, has been extraordinarily kind and generous in his sharing of his time, talents, network and access to resources. It is unquestionably certain that without him and his support this project might never have gotten off the ground.

Our cadre of author experts: Dennis Becker, Willie Crawford, Nicole Dean, Reed Floren, Connie Ragen Green, Jane Mark, Susanne Myers, Rachel Rofe, Marlon Sanders, Tahir Shaw, and Dr. Mani Sivasubramanian,, have all been incredibly kind in welcoming us into the "Webpreneurial Family." They have all privately shared their own insights and reflections with us, shared some of the life, work and personal challenges they have experienced, and made us truly like part of their world. While we were novices at the Internet Marketing industry, each of the authors were open hearted enough to recognize we brought our own unique areas of expertise; they welcomed us, respected us, and were generous enough to work with us on this project. Their advice and support has been wonderful.

While this book project was done entirely on a shoestring budget, a few people were brought in to save Dick and I from ourselves, teaching us the most valuable lesson - learn what you need to do, versus what to outsource. Michael Worthington and Bob Knowles both jumped in feet first to ensure the details of web, graphics, and video were all handled so that we could continue focusing on the book. Cody Jones and Judi Miller of Infusionsoft also took painstaking steps to accelerate their production process, to help make the launch of the book as smooth as possible from their end, in spite dealing with our own editorial schedules, time constraints and fanatical need to understand the customer experience we were creating with them. Janean Jorgensen and Allen at eB Format provided additional last minute support and advice with the completely foreign processes of audio and e-book production and rendering.

Lastly, and certainly not least, we also wish to publically acknowledge our friends and family who have been troopers and really worked to be supportive during this time. The last time anyone saw either of us so engrossed in a project like this certainly would have been during each of our dissertations; and for most of our families and friends, surely they thought that would be the last time we'd be so absorbed in such a project. (Little did we all know!) Thank you, too, for accepting our temporary absences these last few months.

Drs. Christina McCale and Richard D. Moody
McMoody Crawford, LLC
Olympia, Washington

October 6, 2011

EDITORS' FOREWORD

By Dr. Christina McCale and Dr. Richard D. Moody

In the Spring of 2011, we started our own initial exploration of the explosively growing and evolving market of online business. This wasn't a world that was foreign to either of us. Dr. Moody had spent almost a decade at Apple in corporate marketing, strategy and planning in the education market. Dr. McCale had a background from AT&T corporate in helping small and mid-sized businesses learn how to use emerging Internet technologies to improve their businesses. We both considered ourselves pretty web-savvy people. We had been responsible for massive web presences, technology-based communications, and knowing that we had to keep up with the changing options and role of technology in order to be successful.

We had also each pursued our own doctoral programs while working in a corporate environment. We understood the continuum between the development of theory and how that theory eventually plays itself out in the market place.

We each had been pioneers in our own rights in doing many things that webpreneurs and infopreneurs now do today.

Why we did this research
Our curiosity was piqued not purely from a scientific perspective though. Our respective roles in education -- Dick's in the non-profit association world of groups who advocate for the investment in our public education system, and Chris' role as a university professor -- added to our interest in the online arena. What are we doing as a society, as an educational system, to best prepare our students to participate in what Daniel Pink called "The Free Agent Nation" of entrepreneurs, webpreneurs, infopreneurs, writers, authors, affiliates and consultants?

And to be honest, our curiosity was also piqued from a not-so-altruistic perspective. We both had been battered about in the economic tsunami of the 2000s. Bedraggled and a little water logged, we both were looking to construct a new life - but a life that held true to who WE were - intellectuals, academics, writers, researchers, and business professionals who were already steeped in processes and systems understanding.

How we began our research
There is a whole body of qualitative research processes that allow for the

researchers to be participants in the study as well. We began our research by starting simply: getting on mailing lists, reading offers, listening to webinars, visiting websites, going to community forums like The Warrior Forum. We were the researcher-equivalent of the kids who sat in the back of the classroom in high school. We were quiet. We sat. We listened. We assessed and learned. We compared notes. We bought products that were valuable and we bought products that were utter and complete junk.

We started noticing and tracking trends: how certain webpreneurs were consistent in who they were, what they believed and how they treated their fans or followers consistently from one email to the next webinar to the post-sale experience. We started noting who seemed to be "self appointed gurus" versus those who even other webpreneurs respected. We tracked who seemed to play it straight, who seemed to hold integrity above making a fast buck, who really did know what they were talking about, and who had lived the test of longevity.

During this time, we, too, were asking ourselves many of the questions, experiencing many of the situations, and grappling with many of the concerns outlined in the chapters of this book. We finally had to ask ourselves: "We're a pretty intelligent pair of people with an above average background of business experiences and understanding of technology. If _we_ are struggling to assess who to listen to in this maze of information ... then what's the average consumer's experience like?

In context: The broader market
The urban legend, which has actually been unscientifically supported from time to time by various sources, is that less than 3% of all people who start a business online ever make a single dollar. Their business never gets out of the red. They never recoup their investment. Those are pretty dismal realities: not only did these would-be webpreneurs not make their lives better, but for many, they actually made it worse through the additional expenses, home-life tensions and personal struggles they weathered in the process.

That means, in an economy where:
- more than 25 million Americans are unemployed or under-employed (Huffington Post),
- there is net 0 job creation as recent as recent as August of 2011 (MSNBC),
- 8.8% of all student loans default (Chronicle of Higher Education), and
- the poverty rate has hit its highest rates (15.1% or 46.2 million Americans) since 1981 (MSNBC)
- There are people who are desperate to find opportunity to create a better

life for themselves and their families.

As Arianna Huffington of the Huffington Post stated:

"With the toll that the job crisis is taking on the lives of millions of people in this country -- from college graduates who can't get jobs to middle class families being thrown out of their homes -- this is a Category 5 disaster. In extreme cases, financial desperation has even been a reported cause in suicides." (8/30/11)

For our service men and women, the unemployment rate lingers even higher - 19% among junior enlisted troops according to US Dept of Defense research. It seems cruel that after risking life and limb for their country, our troops are returning to an economy that has no way of helping them, and little hope of returning the favor of their sacrifice with new economic opportunity.

Further, there is an entire generation of college-age students who are either foregoing university all together, or downsizing their higher education aspirations from private college experience to state schools; from state schools to community colleges. Traumatized by the economy, this generation will be watch-worthy: knowing that their parents, who also have lost jobs and assets in this economy, have no way to help them, many of these would-be college students are now asking themselves is the risk of mounting tens of thousands of dollars of debt really worth the risk of still not being able to find a job after graduation?

So multiple target audiences: the under- and unemployed, returning military, and an entire youth market of would-have-been college students could all be struggling with the exact same questions we were asking ourselves: but doing it under the duress of financial hardship and loss.

Our partner

In our research, one name consistently showed up among all the Internet marketers we observed as being extraordinarily reputable, ethical, knowledgeable and successful: Willie Crawford. After gathering more research about Willie, his business practices, products, and reputation, we made one proposal - one pitch - to Willie with a proposition: We think people need help. We think that help extends beyond the typical Internet Marketer's reach. Would you want to work with a pair of newbies?

He said yes. Much to our delight, joy, and amazement.

Willie became, for all intents and purposes the "screener." As a webpreneur who had been around since 1995, he's seen, met, mentored, or done business with the vast majority of successful, reputable webpreneurs. There are a lot of amazing webpreneurs who, due to other commitments, timing, business or family demands, simply chose not to be in this particular installment of this book series. We anxiously look forward to gathering their thoughts and including them in the future installments of The McMoodyCrawford Series: Start Your Internet Business.

At the same time, Willie has become our own personal guru to whom we owe much more than just mere gratitude. He taught us so much more than just the nature of the Internet marketing industry and culture.

Our author experts

Each author expert was given the topic, "If you knew then what you know now - what three things would you do differently in starting your business?" Most had problems limiting themselves to just three things. To ensure the book's results would be "agenda-free" we ensured that no coaching, encouragement, questioning or orchestration by either of us took place. We wanted them, without prompting, to disclose what they felt were the most important things they wished they'd known.

The trends, correlation, similarities and results of this process are discussed in the last chapter of this book.

36 THINGS YOU NEED TO KNOW NOW

Eleven highly successful webpreneurs were asked to share what were the three things they wish they'd know when they first started their web-based businesses. Some offered more than three. Some suggestions were overlaps from other authors. But through content analysis, these international expert authors have provided a total of 36 pieces of advice, focused in four key areas: business practices, marketing, operations and keeping your sanity.

The 36 Things You Should Know Before Starting Your Business are:

Business Practices
1. "Build it and they will come" doesn't work. The real work just begins once the product is developed, the book is written, or the website is launched.
2. Create compelling, interesting content that your customers value.
3. Get more customers to buy at your business.
4. Get your customers to spend more at your business.
5. Get more customers to buy more frequently at your business.
6. Failure is part of the entrepreneurial experience. Learn from your failures.
7. Learn to focus your efforts so that you are working on only what truly matters in your business.
8. Perfection is impossible. Good enough really is "good enough."
9. Strive for incremental progress towards your goals on a daily basis.
10. One size does not fit all: Understand you are developing a holistic, integrated business where you have multiple offers that you have leveraged across your information base as well as multi-purposed in ways to meet your customers' needs. Your business, by its very nature, will be different from anyone else's – if you've done your homework.
11. Keep things simple, especially when you're starting out.
12. Know "enough" about your business to be successful. You'll find areas in which you'll, of course, become an expert. But if you wait until you "know enough" to start your business, at the pace in which business changes, you'll never really know "enough."
13. Master the principles of sales: How to make sales, how to engage customers, how to retain customers, and how to grow your relationship with them.
14. Learn to leverage your assets: your network, knowledge, processes, and creativity. Leverage everything to your advantage in the service of your customer.
15. Strive to plan how to make your business profitable from Day 1. Get

very comfortable with understanding the flow of your revenue and what you need to operate your business.

16. Raving customers are invaluable. Thank your customers who are willing to refer their friends to you. Word of mouth advertising is still the holy grail of marketing.
17. There's no reward without risk. Make calculated risks - but take them.
18. Business in the Internet age is changing at an unprecedented rate. Invest in yourself on a regular basis; learn to adapt quickly, how to monitor your environment, and how to assess new opportunities.
19. Measuring and tracking results are vital: It helps you measure the performance of your business on every level.
20. Do not delay in starting a customer list.

Marketing

21. Don't under estimate the power of Article Marketing
22. Never forget Blogging - both on your own site, being a guest blogger, and commenting on other people's blogs.
23. Build your brand. Who are you? What do you want to be known for? What will your company be about?
24. Forum Posting is a great way to expose people to your firm at little cost. Just remember - add value to their lives first, and do it multiple times, before talking about you.
25. Social Media is on the rise: Ignore it at your peril.
26. Video Marketing is a powerful way to connect with your customers and do better in your SEO efforts.
27. Viral Reports can be a powerful mechanism for generating traffic, building your customer list, and bolstering your own credibility on a given topic.

Operations

28. Back-up everything; your data is only as good as your last back up.
29. Set goals or else you risk being directionless and taking twice as long to attain the level of success you desire.
30. Learn to outsource that which does not require you personally doing it.
31. Partnering, either in the form of joint ventures or affiliates, can be a lifesaver for a new web-based business.
32. Take control of your day. Plan what needs to be done, and prioritize those things that need to be done so that they get done.
33. There are no super powers needed to be a success at Internet Marketing: Everyone has the power. It just takes work, dedication, and paying attention to the advice of people like these expert authors.

Keeping your sanity

34. TMI (Too Much Information) also applies to your business in the form of information overload. Focus on what you have to know to be successful.

35. Make a point of getting involved in your new industry or "community" through live, in person events, webinars, etc. People like knowing the "personality" behind the name.

36. Remember - you're human. Design your business to meet your personal needs and life situation. Your business is there to serve you, not for you to serve your business.

ABOUT DENNIS BECKER

Dennis Becker began his Internet marketing career in 1998 by selling on eBay while still running a full time retail business. Beginning in 2002, he became interested in Internet marketing, and spent three years trying virtually everything with dismal results.

One day, frustrated and beat, but unwilling to quit, he devised a new strategy to simplify the process, starting with a mindset makeover. That strategy changed his life, and he wrote about it in the classic Five Bucks a Day.

He also opened an "Insider's Club" in 2007, to help more experienced Internet Marketers achieve their first $1000/day of profits by following proven and sometimes little-appreciated business models to receive amazing results.

Dennis has been involved in a huge number of development projects, but the ones he's best known for include:

- Earn1kaDay.com – the Internet marketer's Insiders Club where we share tips, tactics, success strategies, and disseminate cutting edge information about 12 different business models.
- 5 Bucks a Day – This is how Earn1KADay was born. Learn the techniques that, inspired by a 5-dollar bill, took his Internet marketing income from $30 a day to $700 a day in less than a year.
- And the sequel, 5 Bucks a Day Revisited, written 5 years later, to that evergreen classic.
- Action Enforcer – The desktop application that will bring you more focus and let you get more done in less time than you ever imagined.
- Product Drop – The top destination for Internet marketers to get their hands on a boatload of quality products for one low monthly price.

1

HOW FOCUS AND NOT BEING AFRAID
TO FAIL MADE MAGIC HAPPEN

by DENNIS BECKER
www.earn1kaday.com

When I started marketing on the Internet, I had a heck of a time getting any traction. In fact, I guess I could have been called at the time "a miserable failure."

There, I said it.

That was really frustrating because I had started successful small businesses twice before, without a problem. One was a software consulting company, the other was a small retail store.

Since I had a background in computers and technical things, it frustrated me no end to go three years without making any money online.

That's when I sat down and did a "check up from the neck up" and realized it wasn't me, it wasn't the Internet, it was more than that...

Actually, I guess it <u>was</u> me, or at least my mental approach, and once I got that tweaked, success happened.

These ideas are things that I wish I would have realized years earlier, and would love to pass on to others who are enduring similar frustrations.

Focus is essential

My biggest problem was lack of focus.

For three years I tried everything. All of the things I tried had been taught by someone as sure-fired ways to be successful, but unfortunately they didn't work for me.

As I look back five years later, I notice that the problem was that I would give something a few days, perhaps up to a week, to work, and then I'd move on to something else, never allowing the first plan to do its thing.

It's like if you put a bag of microwavable popcorn into the microwave, press the button. After 30 seconds, you decide nothing's happening, so you stop it, throw the bag away, and try another bag.

But let the bag of popcorn go for the whole three minutes, and magic happens.

So when I started focusing on projects, and giving them a chance to work, magic happened.

I coach quite a lot of people in my Internet forums, and this is the #1 problem I see, time after time. Someone tries something, it doesn't work immediately, and they give up.

Or, they do something that has a good chance of making them some money. They put their site, or their article, or their video, or whatever on the web somewhere, and then they just sit back and wait for the money to come in.

That's all well and good, but while they're waiting, they're doing nothing except watching, and thinking, and wondering "when it will start working?"

Some things you do will take time. So while that time is ticking away, people should be doing other things, so that once the first item starts bringing in revenue, you've already built 10 more things that are in their early stages of development.

For example, when I was first starting out, I was putting together ugly little web sites with affiliate links on them, ugly but still useful to the people who had landed on the pages, or so I thought. Since I was able to build these sites quickly, I didn't worry about whether any individual niche that I was targeting would make a lot of money. Rather, I just wanted to get as big a footprint out onto the web as possible. Some of these sites did very well, some flopped. The thing is, I was mainly focused on the task to build, build, and build, rather than build and wait to see what happened. By doing this, one site I built, that I probably wouldn't have even have dreamed of putting together if I had analyzed it first, made me a profit of over $250 per day.

"Good enough" is good enough

Now don't get me wrong. I love it when things I purchase work right out of the box as they're supposed to, and there's not a typo to be found in the user guide.

And people in certain industries should completely ignore this advice... for example: surgeons, nurses, airline pilots, parachute packers... and a few more.

But my advice to me, who creates mainly information products, and people like me, is that not everything has to be perfect.

Don't get me wrong, I like the information to be excellent, but there are other parts of the process that don't need to be.

The sales page for the product doesn't have to have the most wonderful graphics in the world. The user guide, if it has a typo or a grammatical error, won't hurt anyone. There are other components of a product that can likewise be dealt with after a product is launched.

Think about this. If Bill Gates and crew had waited until everything was perfect in Windows, including absolutely no bugs, no ambiguities in the user manuals, no flaw at all, what would have happened?

There would be no Windows, because it would never have been perfect.

I'd rather have Windows that works pretty much all the time, than not have it at all. Without Windows, the world certainly would be different, agreed? It's made a major impact on every part of our lives, regardless of whether or not some people think that there might be better operating systems available, most of which came after Windows blazed the trail and created a mass-market industry.

So, good enough can be good enough.

As an Internet marketer, I consider it my duty to provide information and encouragement that helps people become more successful in their Internet marketing endeavors. My web pages might be a little ugly to some. There might be a spelling error here and there. My videos and audios certainly aren't studio quality and could be improved a million times over.

But people can, and do get, valuable information from what I do, and to me, that's what I want to happen.

Failure is your friend

This was a huge breakthrough for me once I realized it, and if I would have figured this out many years ago, I would have saved a lot of struggle.

Not everything you do will be successful, in fact probably most things you do won't be successful, at least not the first time.

That doesn't mean give up.

That means, keep going because you're a step closer to succeeding.

Thomas Edison failed how many times in perfecting his light bulb? 10,000? How many people would have kept going that long? How many people would have kept going after five?

I see so many people that give up after one attempt that doesn't work. One attempt!

Here's a sports analogy that I like to use, which might not mean as much if you're not from the U.S. or Canada, but you'll get the idea.

A professional baseball player in the major leagues, who has a .300 batting average, is considered a star, quite likely will be elected to the Baseball Hall of Fame at the end of his career, and during his career will earn upwards of $10-20 million per year.

A .333 batting average means that he averages about 3 hits every 10 times to bat. Or, in other words, he fails about 7 out of every 10 attempts.

And he's a star!

So don't expect that everything you do will work the first time out, and keep plugging.

There's a fine line though: what should you keep plugging at? The thing that has been failing?

No, not necessarily, and it depends. Though I just talked about Thomas Edison, personally I don't want to devote years of my life to experimenting at relatively trivial tasks that might or might not make me money (no, I'm not saying that Edison's experiments were trivial, I'm saying that most of _mine_ are). I want to give each project I work on a chance to work, and if it doesn't I'll move on to something else.

Where's that fine line? When do you stop and move on?

There's an old, hit Country song that says "know when to hold 'em and know when to fold 'em," referring to the game of poker, but equally applicable to life and business.

Knowing when to fold them is an art that comes from experience.

In Internet marketing, there is a term "bright shiny object" (BSO). Many people (like me when I wasn't focusing on anything, like I mentioned before), have the BSO syndrome where we buy a training course or report that supposedly will teach us how to do something that could make us money.

BSO-followers pursue that path until another BSO comes along to catch our eye – which they do every few days at least -- and then move on to the next thing.

Going that route, without focus, is hazardous to your wealth, and should be avoided.

Give things a chance: focus on things until you can get them completed before moving on. You'll be glad you did.

Which brings me to my next lesson that I wish someone would have taught me long ago:

You might already know enough
Yes, if you've been around a while, you might already know enough, without buying another BSO, to be successful in your chosen career.

That's why I was so frustrated in the beginning. I thought that I was bright enough, I had built successful businesses before, I worked hard, I invested in things to build a new online business, but it wasn't working.

When I realized that I already knew enough to be successful, and stopped chasing BSO's, things started to take off, as if by magic.

I'm not saying quit learning. What I'm saying is that if you're using "I don't know enough yet" as an excuse to not move forward, to not create that product (report, video course, white paper, software program, whatever), then you might just be afraid of failure.

It all boils down to procrastination sometimes.

People who put off starting or finishing a project are often just afraid. Afraid of failure, afraid of rejection, afraid they'll lose hope.

Yeah, that's a big one... afraid to lose hope.

You've been working and dreaming of doing something to make you rich and/or famous, and you're afraid that it won't.

You're afraid of the verdict.

So you tweak, and you put off, and you add features, and you do anything you can to avoid an answer.

Like when I was in school, I was painfully shy. There were girls that I really wanted to get to know, and I'd think... tomorrow I'll walk up to her and talk to her and maybe she'll like me.

Tomorrow would come, and I'd find an excuse... I have to do an assignment first, I promised a friend I'd meet him after class, it's raining and she's probably in a bad mood... Whatever. I was just afraid of being shot down and losing hope.

Not appreciating at the time that two things could happen if I just talked to her: she could become my new best friend, or she could say to bug off.

Is the second scenario worse than not doing anything? No, in fact it's better, because though I would lose hope with that person, I get to move on and seek out someone else instead.

It is the same with creating products, or searching for a job, or whatever it is that you do.

I got a little off track here, but the whole point of "you might already know enough" is the same as "good enough is good enough", actually, and is meant to encourage you to just start something.

Additionally, if you don't already know enough to write about a topic, or to create a product, or to build a web site that might make money, it doesn't always take that long to develop that expertise.

You don't have to know everything about something to be an expert, you just need to know more about it than your audience.

Knowing stuff can come from research, and I'm sure you've heard of the best research tool in the world... Google.

There are hundreds of millions of English speaking people with Internet access, don't you think you could learn more about something than most of those people know?

Do I think you can be an expert on weight loss, alleviating acne, credit repair, or some of the more competitive topics, and make a fortune?

No, probably not, but feel free to try. Don't let me talk you out of it.

Somebody new makes money in those niches on a regular basis, why not you? I'd try something less competitive myself, but that's just me, it doesn't have to be you.

There are tens of thousands of smaller, less competitive niches that you can easily find (just search for some obvious ones, "how to do it" is out of the scope of this chapter, but it's not difficult). Or you can search eBay, about.com, magazines, or your local newspaper.

That's just for starters.

You can become an expert if you're willing to devote 40+ hours to it. Not THE expert who goes on a book tour, or THE expert who gets nominated for awards, but a relative expert who can provide quality information to people, and make money doing it.

Forty hours or so, more or less, and you can be an "enough" expert. Consider this: 40 hours or so of research, 10 to 20 hours to distill that research into a report, convert it to a downloadable report, or even upload it to the Kindle platform, and you can be making money or establishing your credibility as a

published author.

You ARE willing to work more than 40 hours in a week if it means changing your life, right?

Remember, people will pay money for what you know. I'm convinced, even though I might not know you personally, that you know something that, if written down and put into a report format, people will pay for.

Which brings me to my next point:

Incremental progress
Along with "failure is your friend" is the incremental progress theory. When you're doing things to reach a goal, it's never a straight path to success.

There will be setbacks along the way, so be prepared, and don't get all frustrated.

Remember, two steps forward and one step back, is better than no steps forward.

There's a law of nature called the "law of momentum." It says that an object in motion will remain in motion until acted upon by an outside force, and an object at rest will remain at rest.

If you're moving in a direction, even if you're occasionally failing, you're better off than if you're sitting around doing nothing.

Again, not everything will work all of the time for everyone.

Incremental progress... so important.

I know a lot of people don't have a lot of time to do major things, but that doesn't matter at all.

I tell people who follow me that if nothing else, if they can devote just a half hour a day to something that's important to them, that's enough.

Spend 30 minutes of focused effort on a project. By focused I mean no surfing the 'net, no phone calls, and no instant messaging systems to distract you. Just lock yourself in a room somewhere where you can't be disturbed for 30 minutes each and every day.

That's not so hard, is it?

At the end of a year, those 365 half-hours add up to 182.5 hours, which is the equivalent of four-and-a-half full work weeks.

Novels can be written in that amount of time. Great works of art can be produced if you have the talent for it. Lot's of products. Expertise in several areas can be learned by reading books or whatever's necessary.

One small step, each and every day, 30 minutes at a time, and at the end of a year, if not a lot sooner, your life can be changed (and maybe that of people who consume whatever your product is).

Now for those that tell me they don't have 30 minutes a day even...

Sigh. I'll bet you do. Everybody has the same 24 hours, no more, no less.

Watch 30 minutes less television. Get up earlier in the morning, or go to bed later. Surely you can come up with 30 minutes somewhere in each day, if not more, to make incremental progress towards your dream project.

I know you can do it, because I can, I have, other people could, other people have, and that brings me to another point.

If he (or she) can do it, I can do it
When I was in my worst period, nothing working, frustration, no focus, etc., I was a member of an online membership site, run by three people who were each successful in their own area of expertise.

I started following one guy in particular, who was using pay-per-click methods to make money.

Now, I'd tried that in the past, and it never worked for me. In fact, it was one of the many things that I had given up on.

It was probably a combination of not doing it right, but also being stubborn about hanging on to hope with a vendor that wasn't meant to be successful. In other words, not "knowing when to fold 'em".

So I started following this guy, and he seemed real and legitimate to me, and in the back of my mind, I said "if he can do this, I can do this."

So I started doing what he was doing, and you know what? I started succeeding like he was.

From that point on, I was wildly successful with those pay-per-click campaigns, though of course some didn't work. It was always part of the game then that maybe one out of 10 campaigns would work, the rest wouldn't, so knowing when to fold 'em was a big part of the secret.

Since then, I've always recommended to my followers that they pick one or more mentors to follow. It isn't important if the person they're following knows that they're being followed or not, and in fact, I've never recommended getting a formal relationship like that.

It's actually more beneficial to sit back and observe someone doing what they're doing in their normal state, because if they try to tell you what to do, like a paid coach might, they tend to leave out steps.

Being able to watch what people do, rather than just listen to what they say, is important... "Do as they do, not as they say".

Summary

Ah, if I would have only known these things just three years sooner, simple things like focusing on one thing at a time, doing small things to improve every day, following the right people, not insisting on perfection, and not being afraid to fail, I could have built a successful online business years sooner than I did.

Thank goodness I didn't give up. I'll admit the temptation was great, because I never had an urge to be as stubborn as Thomas Edison. Luckily, I didn't have to.

Now it's your turn. Good luck.

Editors' note

The Internet has warped much of what we understand about time: Everything on the Internet is instantaneously available. Like turning on a faucet or flipping a switch: The information just immediately flows to us.

But the immediacy or "instant on" nature of the Internet has done entrepreneurs a disservice. This, coupled with the urban legends of building a website in one day and becoming a millionaire the next day, has corrupted what most of us know to be true about business.

Business -- whether it's a storefront on Main Street or on the web - requires effort, planning, processes, and TIME. Time to do the prep work and then time to let the business have a chance to grow.

Many self-proclaimed gurus will tell new webpreneurs to "just do something. Get it out there, it doesn't matter if it's pretty. Just get it out there and if you're going to fail, fail quickly so you can move on to the success that's right around the corner."

The problem is, this advice ignores what we know to be true: all things take time.
This urban legend advice ignores that there are varying levels of success. Not every book is a best seller. Not every movie is a blockbuster. Web-based products (or companies) are no different. But many of the so-called "experts" would have you believe that if your products aren't multi-million dollar successes, then YOU must be doing something wrong.

As Dennis shows us, giving yourself time to work the real process steps involved in developing a great business is critical. Take time to do your homework -- while not falling victim to "analysis paralysis." Take the time to get a sense of the Internet Marketing/webpreneurial industry. It's a big market! Then, once you have a sense of it, focus, focus, and focus. By really understanding what it is you want to do, or who you want to serve, you can pare down the number of webinars you sit through, or the number of extraneous products you buy, and focus on the key action items and milestones you need to meet in order to be successful.

For more information about this author, or to learn more about how to start your own web-based business, go to www.mcmoodycrawford.com. There you can also sign up for our newsletter and announcements about our upcoming events.

ABOUT WILLIE CRAWFORD

Willie Crawford started his online business in his spare time while still an aircrew member flying C-130 aircraft with the US Air Force.

Six years after building his first website, he retired from a 20-year military career as an Air Force Major, and had by that time built a business paying him a six figure income.

With several million followers/subscribers to his email newsletters and social media channels, he now teaches others how to turn their knowledge into information products that the world will happily pay for. Having written over 2,000 articles, over 60 books in print and electronic formats, and given over 80 live seminar presentations, Willie is now regarded as one of the world's leading Internet marketing and joint venture experts.

He now advises both online and offline business owners on how to leverage Internet technologies.

2

YOUR STRENGTHS MAY NOT BE OBVIOUS: LOOK TO YOUR PAST TO BUILD YOUR FUTURE

by WILLIE CRAWFORD
http://williecrawford.com

Having started building an Internet marketing business in 1996, I am an "old-timer" when compared to many of the recognized online marketing "gurus" you encounter today.

I have had the pleasure of mentoring many of the current crop of experts. Conversely, several of them shared their practical experiences with me, and they have helped to shape how I now run my businesses.

While I didn't realize it at the time, my training started while I was in the North Carolina State University ROTC program while earning my degree in business, and entered the Air Force as an officer immediately following my graduation in 1983. A major factor that has impacted my business success is the 20 years and 10 months that I spent as a military officer, where I was essentially a mid-level manager, who often had to make life-or-death decisions, or decisions that cost millions of dollars. Not making these decisions was often not an option.

Life, including my travels to 47 different countries, spending a lot of time fairly close to the possibility of immediate death, and having to focus or compartmentalize in order to get things done, fashioned me into a leader as well as a manager. After that military career, business is largely a cakewalk, as long as I don't forget those hard-won lessons.

Looking back, if I were starting all over again, here are the three biggest lessons that I know now that I would hope I could somehow understand if just starting out.

Don't be afraid to take calculated risks

Every successful business owner has to take calculated risks, and consequently many of them have had major setbacks. Stepping out of one's comfort zone and starting a business is what makes a person an entrepreneur. The important thing is to think about the challenge and weigh the benefits of the risk before making the jump.

I grew up on a farm, surrounded by "farm-hands" and had no entrepreneurs as role models. Yes, I learned to make decisions, to take risks, and to gamble, but with small stakes.

When I thought of the business world, for some reason I assumed that business owners worked from some vantage point of more perfect information, and that they always knew the correct thing to do. Now, having grown numerous online businesses, that experience has shown me how wrong I was, and how well equipped I already was for building my own businesses by having built confidence and experience in making decisions.

From 1996 through late 2002, I ran my online business from a small home office. I struggled to claim mastery of my niche, and viewed everyone in the world as my competitors. Hence I failed to gain exposure to others, or to acknowledge that I could learn a lot faster from cooperating with them. That all changed in December of 2002 when I was invited to speak at an Internet marketing seminar, and I noticed how freely all of the other speakers shared "the secrets" with each other. These are actually the people who taught me not to fear risk in business.

I wasn't "all in" at this point, and I wasn't sure how those Internet "gurus" viewed a part-timer in their world. However, my "real" job presented some challenges that were really opportunities and training that have helped me reach the goals that I have set, and step towards the new goals that have taken their place.

During my first six years as in Internet marketer, I lived a double life as a soldier, so I don't imagine I was very different from many others who had full-time jobs and part-time businesses. The threat of my job requiring me to have to go anywhere I was directed to go, almost at a moment's notice, did force me to put more things in motion as soon as they popped into my head, since I realized that 24 hours later, I might not have Internet access for weeks!

I learned that risk is a part of life and also that...

Failure isn't the end of the road

For many business owners, failure IS inevitable on your way to success.

That was one of the first lessons that I heard loud and clear as I listened to other more seasoned business experts. I can still hear the voice of Ramon Williamson, a coach who also spoke at the December 2002 seminar, saying, "If you know that you are going to fail, that it's an inevitable part of the process, why not go ahead and get it out of the way?"

Ramon pointed out that many successful people in numerous fields (sports, writing, business, science, etc.) had more failures than successes, but they are remembered for their successes. He pointed out that many leading authors had flops with their first two or three books, or a huge collection of rejection slips.

Consider the world of the inventor, hailed for success. Thomas Edison, who tested thousands of materials for the best filament for the electric light bulb is cited for making the statement that he did not fail in any of those attempts. Rather, he succeeded in learning what would not work.

When people look at me now, they realize that everything that I've done couldn't have been a huge success, yet they consider me enviably successful. The successes usually outweigh or overshadow the failures.

I was also taught that you are not your mistakes! A big reason that more people don't take the necessary risk and do those bold things required to start and run a business is that they feel that if the endeavor fails, then they have failed. I had to learn to detach my personal self-worth for the outcome of projects.

I was taught that often the only real cost of failure is the requirement to admit failure, and that often that's not even necessary.

We, as people, do care what others say and think about us. I had to learn that you are not being constantly watched. I began developing that sense in college sociology courses. As a college student, the courses gave me permission to step back and be the observer, noticing how self-conscious most humans are, and how we are constantly preening.

I eventually concluded that if people are all so busy worrying about how they are being perceived, and then they can't be watching my every move. Others don't spend every waking minute of every day watching you or me. They are too busy watching themselves, and wondering what others are thinking about them.

I learned that life (the universe) often rewards decisiveness, getting things done fast, and being the first to do something. Often, it is much more important to get it done than to get it right.

I also discovered that once you got the rough draft done, you could always go back and edit or revise. Once you get that e-book written, or that software coded, or that website up, you can always go back and improve it. However, the more that you fret over getting it "out there" the more you put off just getting started.

It was actually while I was a young major, in a staff job at Headquarters Pacific Air Forces, in Hawaii, that I learned this lesson. My job involved drafting important documents that were often signed by a 4-star general responsible for a huge theater of operation. My immediate boss taught me to get it flowed out on paper, edit it a few times, and then to send it up the chain. If anyone between the general and me didn't like something about my work, they changed it. However, once I got it off my desk, things were set in motion.

I did have bosses further up the chain-of-command who felt compelled to make minor changes to any document they were asked to review. Upon noticing that the general often signed off on documents that I got to take directly to him, without changing a letter, I concluded that changing others' work was a method that some people used to make themselves feel important. So, I learned not to take that personally, and to detach myself from that outcome.

In that very same job, in Hawaii, I worked with a young lieutenant colonel who was a perfectionist. The general would ask him for information to use in making a decision, and this lieutenant colonel could literally spend weeks making phone calls, sending faxes, etc., to gather the most accurate data possible. When asked how close he was to finishing up the paper or project, he always remarked that he was double-checking some data, or waiting on input from someone else. I learned from watching him that stalling on making a decision, and taking action, while waiting for more perfect data, often only leads to projects never getting finished, or the boss transferring them to others who were more decisive.

As I entered the online world full-time in 2003, with six years of Internet marketing experience already under my belt, I kept hearing over and over again that a product that's not on the market earns you nothing. Having a dozen incomplete projects, close to being released earns you nothing. Having one finished, but imperfect, product on the market and selling earns you infinitely more that dozens of "almosts."

The same lesson expressed another way is also to acknowledge that since not all projects are going to succeed, don't invest everything you have in perfecting any one product. Instead, roll them out fast, and then improve on the proven winners. Private discussions with many of my peers who are also industry leaders revealed that they think the same way.

Learn the value of partnerships
You grow your business fastest and easiest by working with others and leveraging your combined assets.

Before speaking at the first seminar in December of 2002, I basically believed that if my customers bought a competitor's product, then they wouldn't have any money left to buy my product. I saw business as a competition for the customers' finite dollars.

Seasoned speakers at that event explained to me that we don't compete for a bigger percent of the existing pie. Instead, we make the pie bigger for everyone, including the customers, so there's more to go around.

One of my first mentors also pointed out that I was handicapped by a tremendous scarcity mindset. My very first job on the farm was when I was maybe seven years old. A neighbor asked my grandmother if I could help out at the tobacco barn, and I was thrust into the adult world of working -- hard work at that. I worked from 7 am to 7 pm, with a one-hour lunch break, for $4 per day.

As I progressed through life, naturally I got better and better paying jobs, and even the farm jobs were up to $18 per day when I left for college in the fall of 1977. However, what I discovered was that I was stuck at viewing $4 as being equal to one day of my life. So, each time that I spent $4, to my way of thinking, it was the equivalent of exchanging a day of my life.

Being stuck in that scarcity and poverty mindset, I actually found it very hard to spend or risk money when first starting my business.

I was taught that the fastest and easiest way to get over that scarcity and poverty mindset was to see that I had a lot more valued assets than I realized. I was taught to survey what assets I currently had that I was under-utilizing, and that others would value.

I was also forced to face up to the fact that $4 no longer represented the value of a day of my life. Today, I have the audacity to post right on my website that a one-hour phone consultation will cost $800. I offer discounts for purchasing larger blocks of time, but I do encounter people who from-time-to-time, just want an hour of my time.

On leveraging my under-utilized assets, I learned the concept of the joint venture where two or more people working together to accomplish a lot more than they ever could alone. After mastering that concept, I discovered that I could partner with programmers, webmasters, fellow business owners, newspapers. The lesson was that with the value proposition, I could partner with practically anyone.

I learned to look for ways to leverage other people's hidden assets, and eventually started charging for that very service itself. There were so few people who really understood this art, who were also actively working as consultants. So things evolved to the point, that now I get paid 10% of the gross revenue produced from many deals just from introducing the right parties to each other.

If I had to start over again today, that would be what I would focus on because it is possible to broker a deal with literally no product, no website, no email list, or no name recognition. Literally, it is nothing more than the ability to orchestrate successful projects.

There are actually hundreds of people in Internet marketing who have positioned them as joint venture brokers, but most achieve very little success. What they usually fail to master is how to answer the "What's in it for me?" question as they approach people with joint venture proposals.

It's very easy to string together lucrative projects that generate six, seven, and even eight figures very quickly, when you approach it from the perspective of letting the other guy see that you sincerely understand his challenges, and are putting his needs first.

Part of what makes me very effective as a joint venture broker is that I not only put the joint venture partners' interests first, but I also put their customers' interests first.

I won't let a novice, rising Internet marketer do something stupid that will harm his customers and in the long run destroy his business. Lot's of Internet marketers will sell almost anything for a quick buck. I think many of them do this more out of desperation than being "evil," but many will sell very questionable products.

I make it my duty only to approach them with quality products that I've thoroughly investigated, and know will truly benefit their customers. In so doing, I gain an unprecedented level of access to some major industry players, who have learned to rely upon my judgment. Just as importantly, I help to ensure that they take good enough care of their customers that they don't kill the proverbial goose that lays the golden egg.

It's OK to be human
Yes, it really is OK to be human, even to love your customers, and to actually appreciate their quirks.

Over the years, I've watched dozens of marketers, who appeared very successful, burn out and go off to do something that they found more fulfilling. I have observed that several of them went into the ministry for example, and while I don't belittle a person's calling, I did at times joke with them that they were trying to make up for past wrongs.

Marketers who view selling as figuring out a way to convince their customers to buy something that they don't want to buy, often burn out due to the constant struggle.

Marketers who think of their population of customers as "the herd" waiting to be whipped into a buying frenzy, or "lemming" that will follow each other over a cliff (or down a buying trail), often burn out due to the fact that they feel like they are tricking people into buying decisions.

I've learned to absolutely, positively shield myself against burnout by only selling products that I honestly feel benefit everyone that they touch.

I've been approached by dozens of unsavory types who suggested that I hand my unconverted leads over to them, so that they can "work them" and generate additional revenue streams for me. I actually have no doubt that they would be very effective, and make me lots of extra money. However, I've allowed myself to care about my customers more than I do about the money. Many business owners would argue that that's a poor way to run a business, but I would argue that that is the only way to run a business.

One of the things that belief has forced me to do is to acknowledge that I'm dealing with people; recognizing we are all powered by electrical and chemical reactions, that are at times unpredictable and irrational. My long-term success has come partly from me applying what Jay Abraham has termed his "Strategy of Preeminence." That strategy teaches you to care about your customers as much as a loving parent cares about his/her children.

Human interactions are tricky, and I've discovered that the easiest way to make them more productive is to be authentic.

At my very first seminar, as I was giving my presentation, I felt like a rock star in front of that audience. I also felt very much that I was being an actor in a play, expected to live up to a certain standard. People like to follow successful, inspiring leaders, my military training had taught me that, and so had my sales training. So, I felt the need to live up to their expectation, but also saw that as a potential, fatal conflict.

This is an issue that I grappled with many times in my online career. Many new marketers feel that the only way to make sales it to "fake it until you make it." The reason is that if they don't pretend to be more than they are, they won't have the credibility required to make sales.

Experience has proven to me, and to many peers, that authenticity wins in the long run. Part of the reason is that we are chemical/biological/electrical creatures who communicate more non-verbally than verbally. We do give off electrical and chemical messages that are many times more powerful than what we verbalize. So, starting over, I would hope to allow my authentic self to shine through.

Starting over with just those three basic realizations would make building a business easier, and a lot less stressful.

Editors' note

There are a lot of reasons why you might be exploring staring an Internet-based business. In an economy where jobs are scarce, you may be finding it important to create your own opportunity. In the uncertainty of Corporate America, you may need to find your own "golden parachute" - a safety net - in case the worst happens. Or maybe this has been a dream of yours for a long time...?

Whatever the reason, you are your first, biggest asset. Take stock - or inventory - of what you have to offer. Just as Willie can now look back and see that every job he ever had helped him in some way to be more prepared for this career path (even before he knew it was an option), you have skills. You've gathered all kinds of abilities to add value to You, Inc. What are those skills? Those assets? Those abilities? This is a new adventure on your professional career path. Manage it that way.

If fear of failure or competition worries you, then consider changing your frame of mind, just as Willie experienced. You can learn from everyone. Coopertition is a very real option for small business that can't possibly do it all themselves: the idea of us vs. them doesn't necessarily serve the webpreneur well.

The web has created a new, dynamic and organic environment where the best people can come together on a project by project basis, form a "virtual organization" with a clear direction and goal, work together to accomplish that goal and then move on to the next project. In this "Free Agent" model, today's competitor might be your biggest ally in a product launch. Today's colleague could be tomorrow's vender.

Willie's unique perspective on the Internet Market is particularly insightful - he brings parties together to get a product to market that perhaps couldn't be done independent of each other. Take a page from his road map; being more concerned about the goals or who the best people are to work with and less about who's "the competition" or "the enemy." When you're not busy dividing up the world, you might find you have more opportunities and people to work with than you ever could have imagined!

For more information about this author, or to learn more about how to start your own web-based business, go to <u>www.mcmoodycrawford.com</u>. There you can also sign up for our newsletter and announcements about our upcoming events.

ABOUT NICOLE DEAN

Nicole Dean jumps out of bed every morning, excited about teaching others how to make money online. Her goal is to show people that earning a full-time income online is doable — with the right teachers and focus, but you've got to take ACTION in order to get there.

Nicole is an experienced affiliate marketer, publisher and coach helping business owners to discover lasting and successful strategies for marketing and operating their businesses online. In her quest to help businesses soar on the Internet, she also owns Shelancers.com, a site that attracts some of the Internet's top professionals in graphic design, virtual assistance, and website content development. It is becoming an indispensable website for small businesses hungry for short- or long-term expertise to support their online efforts.

Nicole also created and manages a number of websites that include resources for starting and managing a small or home based business; effective website marketing and; online content development. These offer both free advice and e-courses and other services and programs that provide clear information and educational material for small business owners.

Being a busy mom and marketer, Nicole has learned to use the right tool for the job to be more efficient and effective.

35

3

ARE YOU SALLY? OR, ARE YOU SILLY?
SIMPLE STEPS TO SUCCESS

by NICOLE DEAN
www.NicoleontheNet.com

I wasn't born with a business manual in my hand. I asked my mom. She said that she'd have remembered if I had been. She said that a business manual would have stood out to her. Even with all the hoopla of birth going on, she'd have noticed that part.

No, I was born with nothing other than an immediate and intense desire to explore and learn everything that this great big world had to offer me. But, no, I wasn't born with a business manual. And, as I grew, I discovered that I had no innate business talents, skills, or business knowledge of any kind. In fact, in high school and college, I avoided taking any courses that sounded like it might even mention the word business in it. Business was boring. Who wanted to be a banker or lawyer? Not me.

Why do I share this? Because I had *nothing* special that you don't have.

My daddy isn't Donald Trump. I was handed down neither Donald's business know-how, nor his money. I had no big advantage in skills or aptitude that you don't have. I had no big fat inheritance that I invested in my business to make it grow that you don't have.

I was (and am) just… like… you.

And, I'd bet, if you asked the other successful authors of this book, they'd say the exact same thing.

I am very excited to share the three things I wish I'd known sooner. I do have to say that there are a lot more than three on my list that I wish I could share. However, I tried to select the three that would have been the most impactful to me – had I known them sooner.

I debated a lot about which three things to share. Would I share marketing lessons? Should I recommend that you enhance your copywriting skills? Or maybe it would be best to encourage you to outsource sooner?

But, no. I decided to talk about the things that I struggled with the most – which was learning a business mindset and overcoming overwhelm. And, how to get through the tough times.

On that note, the three things I'd like to touch on in this chapter are:
- Goals,
- The Importance of Support, and
- Focus.

1. The two kinds of goals and the magic of each

I'd like to introduce you to the most important thing I've learned in the years that I've been running my own online business. I wish someone had beaten me over the head with this information in 2004 – but instead I had to learn it the hard way. Lucky for you that you don't have to. You were smart enough to buy this book.

There are two types of goals that you need to set. NOW.

The first are your financial goals. That simply means how much money you want to make and how soon you want to make it.

But the other type of goals that are, equally important, possibly even more important, are your lifestyle goals. Your lifestyle goals define what your LIFE will look like during the time you're working towards those goals and as you reach them.

Together these two types of goals work as a treasure map to your dream life.

If you're missing either of them, you will be lost.

Unfortunately, I speak from experience. This is a concept that I missed for my first few years and it really held me back. I think of how much further ahead I could be in my business now if only I had had this revelation way back when.

Financial goals are pretty straight-forward. So, let's talk about lifestyle goals first.

Lifestyle goals to me include the following:
- How many hours will you be working per day and per week?
- How many days off will you have during the year?
- How available will you have to be to the Internet or cell phone for your business?
- Where in the world will you be living?
- How much work stress will you have in your life?
- Will you be accountable to other people or only to yourself?
- Will your significant other be working at home with you?
- Will your kids be working in your business?
- Will you be traveling? How often?
- When you're traveling, will you be enjoying it or trapped to your iPhone?
- What is it that you want?

You have to know where you're headed. Otherwise, the decisions that you're going to make on the way there are going to be wrong.

Yes, you can be making $100,000 per month. But if you're miserable and trapped to your desk, and your butt is twice the size it was six months before, and you're unhealthy, and you're getting diabetic, and your blood pressure is up, then what the heck does the money matter? I hate to be morbid, but money won't do you a whole lot of good if you're dead.

So, this is important: Take care of yourself and make sure that you're making your decisions based upon your lifestyle goals.

What I want you to do right now is to write down your goals, even if you are the only one who will ever see them. If you want to fold them up and stick them in the back of a drawer, so nobody else sees what you wrote down, still do it. The act of putting pen to paper makes it more real than just visualizing your goals while sitting on the couch watching TV.

So, write down your one-, five-, and 10-year goals. Include a dollar amount per month. I also want you to write a description of what your life will look like at that time. How will you spend your time? How will your life be different?

This is important to do now, because it will help you to make decisions every day. When you think about starting a new project, you can look at your financial goals and you might think "Yes, that will help me move toward my financial goals" but then look at your lifestyle goals and think "No, that would trap me to my cell phone and make me miserable". If that's the case, see if you can alter that project so that both goals can be met. These two goals will become your constant guide to help you choose which roads to head down.

Once you have your goals, the end is in sight. Now, start to plan the road to that point: Break it down into monthly goals that you need to accomplish, then weekly goals, then daily goals.

This is hugely important to keep your productivity. While I'm on the subject of productivity let's talk about your day-to-day tasks.

Why a "to-do" or "action" list is important.
Let's take a peek into the workday of two fictitious twins: Silly and Sally.

> Silly's Day: Silly gets up, grabs a cup of coffee and sits down at her desk. She thinks "Hmm... I wonder what I should work on today?" and then wanders off to check email and Twitter while she continues to decide what to work on. Several hours later, it's time for her to get off the computer and she thinks "I didn't get anything productive done! There's never enough time in the day. I just don't understand. I was busy all day!"

> Sally's Day: Sally gets up, grabs a cup of coffee and sits down at her desk. She picks up her action list of 6 items that she wants to get done for the day, and determines which one to tackle first. She then spends some focused time and finishes five of the items on her list. After that she decides that she's almost out of time for the day, so she quickly checks email and Facebook. Then, she makes her list for the next day, making sure to transfer the one item that didn't get done to the new list.

Which one of those days looks more productive to you? It doesn't take an efficiency expert to see that Sally is much more productive and gets more done (and probably makes a heck of a lot more money than Silly does).

When all things are even – Sally is the winner by a long shot.

So are you Sally? Or are you Silly?

Now, I could talk forever about this topic, but I'm trying to stay very focused on what works the best, so I'll try to keep it short.

Make your action list at night

A tip that I learned a while ago is to make your to-do list at the end of your workday. So, at the end of today, I will make my to-do list for tomorrow.

Why is this such an important tip? Well, just think of the alternative. Did you notice that Sally sat down and was immediately able to jump into her action list? Not Silly. She had to sit and try to remember where she left off the day before. That's not exactly the way to start off a productive day, is it?

Keep it simple. Keep it short.

I'm easily overwhelmed, so I like to write my action list for the day on a standard index card and limit it to six money-making tasks that I believe I can get *done* that day. I do not list everything that I need to do on that list or I'd just look at it and freeze and wander off to Facebook or grab someone on Instant Messenger to chat and stay "busy" but not "productive".

I've tried numerous systems, including mind mapping, expensive day planning systems, and complicated computer programs. And, yes, I do use a larger system for planning my overall business.

HOWEVER… for the daily "to do" list tasks, I have found that simplicity is the one trick that works best for me. So, I run back to the simplicity of my wonderful index cards and my list of six items on it every time, simply because it works.

By keeping my list of six tasks in front of me and having it ready for me in the morning, I find that I accomplish two things:

> I get more accomplished in my day. This is pretty self-explanatory.
>
> I know when I'm done. If you don't have a daily action list, how will you ever know when to leave your computer? There will always be more to do… Without my action list, I could grow roots to my swivel chair within a week's time.

Finding your way back

A daily action list also serves a busy home entrepreneur in one other way. When I get interrupted (and I do, often), I can very easily find my way back to productivity with one glance. Which of the six things was I working on? If I wasn't any of them... well, then I was off track to begin with and I just busted myself.

When I didn't have my daily list, I would have two major problems for an entrepreneur. I'd be unproductive. And, I'd be unproductive for a <u>really</u> long time, since I didn't know when I was done for the day. I know it sounds silly, but it's practically an epidemic of colossal proportions when talking with online entrepreneurs.

The Moral of the Story? Don't be Silly! Get your Work Done.

I'd like you to try it. Buy some index cards and keep them by your desk. Every day before you call it "quitting time" make your list of 6 items to do the next day. Start your day with that list. See how much more work you get done and you can thank me later.

2. The one essential thing you must have if you want to survive in business

There is only one essential thing that will make or break you in business: People.

You have to have a support group that understands what you do for a living. It's difficult running your own business, whether online of offline, and without support, you will struggle.

You need people. A support system of people who will be able to reach down to pick you up when you fall and they'll dust off your britches and put you back on your feet. And, for sure you will fall on occasion. It's part of life. You may be a very resilient person, in general, and that's great. But, there will be days when you just really want to throw in the towel. If you don't have a supportive network of people who understand – you just might.

Now, when I say that you need people, I'm not talking about a sister, your spouse, or a long-time friend. When I'm having one of those days, I used to try to turn to my husband or one my friends, but they don't get it. While those people very likely may have your best interests at heart and may love you dearly, they can't understand how you feel.

It's not their business; it's yours.

It's not their passion; it's yours.

They can't relate to the depth and range of feelings that you're feeling at that moment whether it's disappointment, feeling lost or stupid, whatever emotion that you're feeling. They'll look at you with glazed over eyes. You must have people that actually understand how you feel, how you deeply you feel it, and how your emotions are tied to your business.

Yes, you can admit it. As business owners, our business' successes and failures are directly tied to our own personal identity. The success of your business is tied into your own self worth. If your business fails, then what does that say about you? These are all the crazy things that run through our heads. Our business becomes an extension of us.

At a time like that is when you've got to have someone that actually knows what you're going through. If you call your offline friends and try to talk to them about it, they're going to try to be supportive, but what they often will do is …. well, be the exact opposite.

Their instinct is to try to protect you, which usually means that they start to say all the reasons why something didn't work other than either you're doing it wrong or maybe you're not trying hard enough. They'll say, "Oh, well that's a scam, of course that won't work." They'll give you 100 reasons why it wouldn't work other than, "maybe you're not focused enough," which is what a true friend will tell you after they rub your shoulders.

Or, they'll just cheer you on, which isn't helpful either. Sometimes you need a kick in the shorts to move ahead.

Either way, they usually can't offer any practical business advice that will move you forward.

You need to have somebody who's going to pat you on the back and say, "It's okay. I've had those days too. Now, what are we going to do about it? How focused are you? What's your biggest money maker? Let's focus on that."

But, there's a catch. The people that I'm referring to, that you need to surround yourself with, need to meet certain criteria.

Your inner circle should consist of people who are generally positive types of people, of course. However, they should have also reached a certain level of success themselves. Even more ideal is if they have a variety of strengths and skills – hopefully some that are different than your own. That will help you when you get stuck. You'll be able to reach out and have someone to ask who can help.

So, take that into consideration. When you ask one of your friends for advice and you're having a bad day, what comes out of their mouth should be something that helps you. They can only do that if they've reached a level of success that's near to you, so they can pull you ahead. Otherwise, they're just pulling you backwards.

Where do you find these people?

First of all, if you're starting off, I recommend hiring a coach if you can in any way afford to. That person may not become the friend that you're looking for, but it will give you a person who you can reach out to and who can help you to move ahead when you get stuck. That person, if she is doing her job, will also motivate you when you need a kick in the shorts, too. Most importantly, that person will be able to understand what you're going through and give you advice when you need it, cheer you on when you're down, and get you pointed back in the right direction when you leave your path.

The other best place to get to know people that you can develop a business friendship with is at live events. There are some absolutely fabulous conferences for this industry that attract amazing people. (Of course, some of the events are complete bombs, too, so check out the preconference agenda for topics relevant to your field, from people you trust and want to learn from.) If you can find a good conference near your home, go to it. I try to attend six events per year. That's a nice balance for me. Why would I travel six times per year for business when I don't have to? Because each and every one has directly increased my revenue in some way.

Where you do not want to find your Inner Circle.

While we're on the topic, there are two places where you do not want to find your inner circle. First, avoid free forums. Usually the people who are hanging there are not DOING anything in their businesses. They're playing around although they may talk big.

If you're part of a networking forum where you have to pay to be a member, then that's completely different. Those people have shown that they're serious about their businesses by investing money, even if it's only a small amount. You can make great connections there.

The other place that I'd avoid is Social Networking sites. I would not recommend connecting on a serious level very quickly with anyone you meet on Facebook or LinkedIn or Twitter. Again, those oftentimes are the types of people in business who are talking the talk, but not walking the walk.

3. Multiplication through subtraction

I coined the phrase "Multiplication Through Subtraction" a while ago when I first realized that business has some funky math that doesn't seem to work in the real world.

I discovered that the more I subtracted from my business and my mental clutter, the more I multiplied my income.

Let me explain.

When you first start exploring the world of web business, it's pretty overwhelming. As you dig in further, you realize that it's extremely overwhelming and there's no possible way on earth that you could ever learn or actually do everything that they say you need to do in order to run a web business in your lifetime.

Am I right? Of course.

I mean let's just look at a few web marketing tactics:
• Article marketing
• Press releases
• Podcast interviews
• Video marketing
• Paid advertising
• Guest blogging,
• Publishing on the Kindle
• The list goes on...

Is your brain tired yet? Now, picture yourself trying to do each of those things each month. There are major two problems with that:
• Problem 1: You'd burn out.
• Problem 2: You wouldn't be effective or efficient at (or be able to MASTER) anything.

Let me illustrate with a story of Stacy and Susan.

Stacy is a "multi-tasker" who likes to do all kinds of things in her business. She read on a blog somewhere that she had to diversify her marketing so this is a snapshot of what her month looked like. She wrote one article and figured out how to submit it (after some tears and chocolate), the next week wrote one press release and figured out how to submit it (after more chocolate), the next week recorded one video and submitted it (after taking a shower, doing her makeup and recording several tries, that one video took a full day), and she is now trying to figure out podcasting. She's exhausted, confused, and doesn't understand how to do any of the above very well. Most importantly she feels defeated and deflated and discouraged.

Susan, on the other hand, is super focused. She's challenged herself to write one article per day for an entire month, submitting them to a variety of directories and as guest blog posts to popular blogs in her market. At the end of the month, she's not only written 30 articles, but her smart business coach had her plan the articles so that they flow naturally into an e-book that she'll also be selling on her website. Susan is energized and excited about her business.

Can you see how Susan multiplied her income by subtracting options and distractions?

Let me share another example.

Mike learned that niche marketing was the way to go. So, he set up 10 different blogs, each in a different niche from hiking to ferrets, but avoided hiking ferrets since that would just be silly. He sat down and waited for the money to pour in. It didn't. He started to promote each site and got exhausted trying to get exposure for each one on different forums and blogs. He gave up, claiming this "Internet thing" doesn't work.

Compare Mike to Mark:

Mark learned to take a project to profit before expanding. So, he chose one market around his passion and dove into it whole-heartedly. Because he focused on one area of expertise – he became an expert and was asked to write a weekly column for the local paper. He then authored a book and was asked to be a national public speaker about his topic. Mark reached six figures his first year.

So, subtract the noise, and multiply your profits. It works.

Well, that's a wrap for me. I hope these three lessons that I learned were helpful and that it saves you lots of heartache. I'd like to close with my motto "You don't have to be perfect to be profitable."

I'm far from perfect, yet I'm very profitable, so I know it's true.

Go out there and do good things. My business statement is to "Make the Web and the World a Better Place". I challenge you to do the same.

Editors' note

Nicole Dean dispels the myths that most people think (but sometimes dare not say) that successful business people are somehow "special" -- that they are different from us regular mere morals.

Sure, every industry has it's "greats" -- whether it's Michael Jordan or Warren Buffet; it's Steve Jobs or Bono. But there are tons of people who are also successful in those same industries without being THEM. Success is not an "all or nothing" game: there are increments of success (just as meaningful to those who have that success). And yes, you, like Nicole and the rest of our expert authors, can experience that kind of success as well.

So many new webpreneurs run around chasing the latest thing, that they fail to do the homework - the basic steps required of all successful entrepreneurs - that needs to be done. While some self appointed "gurus" might "pooh-pooh" the idea of planning, Nicole brings home the point that "planning and goal setting" in this situation is not the seemingly meaningless, time-sucking exercise so many corporations drag their employees through - only to see little in terms of change at the end of it all.

This kind of planning and goal setting is VITAL. YOU are the captain of your ship. Chart a course - to do that you need a map - or, a plan.

Nicole also refocuses our attention on the importance of balance: while creating that "business plan" having a "LIFE plan" too is vital. The shift from being worker-bee to webpreneur can be pretty jolting. Remember, just as you are designing your web pages, business cards, etc - you are also designing a whole new life for yourself. Getting organized and detailing what you need to do each and every day to be successful is much more fun and rewarding when you realize that YOU are the one reaping the rewards of it at the end

ABOUT REED FLOREN

Reed Floren has been marketing online he was 13 years old (back in 1999), he's now 25 and has never had a "real job" or even gone to college.

Yet, Reed has a following of a couple hundred thousand subscribers and has spoken all over the world including the United States, Canada, England, New Zealand, Australia, Singapore, Malaysia and Hong Kong teaching others how to create Internet businesses on a shoe string budget that can replace your job and give you a lifestyle that up until a few years ago only the super rich and famous could enjoy!

4

SUCCESS IS ALL ABOUT YOUR CUSTOMER STRATEGY: 10 STEPS TO SUCCESS

by REED FLOREN
www.reedfloren.com

When I started I wish I had really put it together that there are only 3 real ways to get more money out of your business.

1. Get more customers
2. Get your customers to spend more on each purchase
3. Get your customers to buy more often

That's really all there is to business, if you can master those three principles you will be further ahead than 99% of the people out there.

I learned this the hard way. For years I kept bouncing around from thing to thing, looking for that shiny object that would make success just happen.

What did I learn? Quit searching for that lottery ticket. You won't find it! Instead focus on one business opportunity at a time and decide if it's the right one for you.

But how do you do that?

Here's how I decided that I should get into Internet marketing.

Rewind back to 1999 and I'm just your typical 13 year old, searching and wondering how I'm going to make money to start hanging out with my friends outside of school.

And then it hits me.

What was in the news every single day at that time?

That's right: the Internet.

So I began searching for ways to start making money online. I mean, come on, who wants to flip burgers at McDonald's when TV and newspapers make it sound like ANYONE can make money online.

Combine this "easy wealth" with knowing that my dad drove three hours a day, waking up at 4:30 am and coming home at 7 pm, so I could go to the school I was in and you can see why the prospect of working from home excited me!

That school provided me with a great opportunity. It had computers, high-speed access, and teachers who, while they didn't know exactly what it was that I was doing, encouraged me to keep trying. I didn't know it at the time, but I had a perfect business incubator environment. In the 8th grade I had a project to build a web site and wrote a book on it. Well, perfect except that I had to change my project because it had the word "sex" in it: "Sex isn't the only thing that sells on the Internet."

Throughout school I kept searching the Internet for ways to make money and I'd haphazardly start one idea only to be seduced by another the next day. If I had only developed a plan and stuck to it, success would have found me a lot faster.

Even in the late 1990's and early 2000's marketers were using tools called auto responders which allow you to collect someone's name and email and send them targeted information and offers into their inbox.

My biggest fear at the time was how I would come up with $20 a month every single month to attempt this idea. In other words I let a measly $20 rob success from me for years!

You see I was on these marketer's lists, receiving their email messages buying some of the offers and reading almost every message they sent me. I was addicted and was quickly becoming an Internet marketing junkie.

Focus on communication
If I could go back to the beginning I would have created some sort of email newsletter that focused on my journey of learning how to develop an income at home part time with little investment and I would have connected with Internet marketer and success gurus to do interviews for my followers.

This brings me to another very important aspect of Internet marketing.

Build trust
You may think that you are just marketing to other computers on the Internet but that isn't the case you are marketing to real world human beings who will make an emotional decision to buy from you if they feel like they know, like and trust you.

What's the easiest way to get people to like you from the start?

Get an endorsement from someone they already know, like and trust.

But how do I do that?

The simplest, fastest and easiest way to connect with the movers and shakers in your industry is to meet them at a seminar or other offline event.

Yes that's right. I said get off your butt and go to a seminar.

Now you usually wouldn't learn a ton by actually attending sessions by the speakers but instead hang around the bar area and buy other marketers a beer. You'll be amazed at the wealth of knowledge you can pick up for just a few dollars, many marketers will lay out their entire business model for you if you know how to ask.

At the seminar, spend your time listening to the others and offering up good information when you can. If you have the capability to help them in any way, do so. Perhaps you are good with sales copy or graphics or programming if they need help in any of those areas offer to help them at no cost.

This is a very small industry and if you are a person who can develop a reputation for going above and beyond and is helpful to others than you will get a lot of friends fast who will love to help you out when the time arises.

Know when to ask for help

The third major thing I wish I could go back and do, would be to know when to ask for help.

Being a stubborn teenager with a major ego problem, I wrongly believed that if I didn't know how to do something and couldn't figure it out quickly then there's no way other people would know the answer to it, so why waste your time asking for assistance? Besides, you wouldn't want to look like you didn't know the answer would you?

Get over yourself, buddy. Nobody likes a know-it-all jerk! Don't be afraid of looking dumb, spending hours doing Google searches, when the answers are out there with people who have experience and are willing to share it.

A major mindset shift happened to me when an gentleman in his 70s came up to me and said "We are all educated idiots" and what I gather that he meant is that there are plenty of things you can teach me and vice versa. In other words, get your head out of your you-know-what... and ask somebody for help from time to time.

Without learning this powerful principle I would have never been able to do the things I've done.

Quite frankly I'm not very good at a lot of areas of Internet marketing but I am good at the areas that tend to develop MASSIVE results FAST and I'm fine with that. That's where my personality lies and that's what I LOVE doing.

But you won't catch me writing highly search engine optimized content anytime soon, since I never seemed to figure it out and found it way too boring.

When I first started writing this chapter I told you that there were only three real ways to make more money from your business.
Get more customers
1. Get more customers
2. Get your customers to spend more on each purchase
3. Get your customers to buy more often

In order to do these three things, here is the plan I suggest you follow if you want to build a successful Internet based information publishing business.

Step 1: Plan out your ideal lifestyle

What is it that you want out of your life? Do you want economic freedom to enjoy new things? Geographic freedom to travel? Time freedom to go anywhere at a moment's notice. Write out what you really want out of your life and how you expect to be living in the next few years. This will make success happen a lot faster!

Step 2: Pick a hot market that you are passionate about

Have you purchased an information product (either online or off) in this market? Here are a couple of ideas... business (Internet marketing), finance (stocks) self-improvement, technology (how to), hobbies (dog training), dating, and the list goes on and on. Just pick one of these that you have a real desire and can picture yourself and your business taking off.

Step 3: Come up with something of value to give away

You don't need to be the end all be all expert on your chosen topic yet but at the very least write or record something that shares what you've learned so far and save your subscribers time by providing interesting information they can put into action TODAY to better improve their life.

Step 4: Do not be afraid to invest in the necessary tools

Of all the types of businesses to start, Internet marketing is one of the cheapest (if not the cheapest) to actually get going and run. Get a domain name, hosting, a way to process payments (PayPal is fine) and an auto responder account. Starting at around $30 per month, you could have all the tools you need to run a part time business that could replace your job!

Step 5: Connect with other marketers

Look at the websites in your niche and focus on finding seminars that would attract movers and shakers in your market to attend. Go to these people with the plan of attack of wanting to be their friend and help them out and you will get a lot more out of it then being the guy that follows someone into the bathroom and tries to get them to promote your product (yes, I've actually seen people do this)

Step 6: Follow-up

After meeting these influential people do what you promised you'd do and see what else you can do to help them out. Once you've developed a rapport with them and know various tidbits about them and their family then you can start working on getting them to help you.

Step 7: Ask for help

Reach out to those marketers that you've befriended and ask them for their feedback on your web site or product and tell them you really value their opinion on it. Many people will gladly help out a friend who simply asks for help.

Step 8: Ask for an interview

Tell your new friends that you'd be honored to interview them for your audience and sell their products or services to your list. If you can get enough of these other marketers on board you can even require that they promote the calls to their own list which will help you build a massive targeted list for free and earn affiliate commissions by promoting others. Now just by doing these interviews your perception in the marketplace is that you are at least on the same level as the person you are interviewing.

Step 9: Promote, promote, and promote

Get the help of your new friends to continue to promote what you are doing and then return the favor by promoting their quality products to your list.

Step 10: Develop a back-end

The real money in Internet marketing is in selling higher priced products and services to your existing clients. Continue to serve your customers interests and they will continue to fill your bank account by trusting you when they want to find a solution to their problems.

If you follow these 10 steps you will avoid the grand majority of mistakes that many marketers make and you'll be able to develop a long-term Internet business which not only can generate almost immediate cash for you know but a lifestyle that only the super rich and famous could afford just a few years ago.

Take action now!

Editors' note

Reed Floren is the epitome of Generation Y (or "Millennials") -- people who were born between 1980 and 2004; up and coming webpreneurs who have grown up with the possibilities of all that the Internet has to offer.

Reed's story is great example of how we as parents, teachers, and systems could be fostering the entrepreneurial spirit of our young people. By channeling their energies into creatively developing business ideas, we could be growing the next generation of Warren Buffetts or Bill Gates' - with even fewer resource obstacles in their way!

The 10 steps Reed outlines capitalizes on the core lessons he - and many of our authors - have learned: establishing trust (which means not only knowing who you are, what your core values are, but also being a "trustable" business person), developing strong communications skills - with everyone from customers to employees to partners - is a non-negotiable. And, not just being willing to do the homework and learn what you need to do - but then taking action and doing it.

For more information about this author, or to learn more about how to start your own web-based business, go to www.mcmoodycrawford.com. There you can also sign up for our newsletter and announcements about our upcoming events.

ABOUT CONNIE RAGEN GREEN

Connie Ragen Green is a former classroom teacher and real estate appraiser who left it all behind to come online in 2006. After 20 years of working 6-7 days a week and missing nearly every special occasion with her family, Connie made the decision to become an online entrepreneur. After struggling during her first year, she has now gone on to teach new online entrepreneurs from around the world how to build a profitable business on the Internet.

Connie has authored five books, speaks at marketing events across the country, and has more than 20 digital products on a variety of topics. Connie teaches new online entrepreneurs how to build a profitable business on the Internet. Claim your free report on "21 Ways To Make Money Online With Your Tiny List" by visiting http://HugeProfitsTinyList.com.

5

HOW 'BURNING THE SHIPS' BLAZED MY PATH FROM TEACHER AND REAL ESTATE AGENT TO THE INTERNET

by CONNIE RAGEN GREEN
http://conniegreen.com/

You've probably heard the saying that "hindsight is 20/20", which means that we would all know exactly what to do in life if we could just go back in time.

This is so true as I think about my decision to start an Internet business back in 2006. If I had known then what I know now about getting started online, my life would have been much easier those first couple of years and I would be much further along in my progress today. We can't turn back the clock, so the next best thing is for me to share the lessons I've learned that would have made the most difference in helping me to accelerate my success and maximize my profits.

First, I'd like to tell you a little bit about myself. I live in southern California, and own homes in both Santa Clarita, north of Los Angeles, and Santa Barbara, less than a mile from the beach. I go back and forth between these two beautiful locations when I'm not traveling all over the country to speak and present at live events.

I'm also very active with several charities and non-profit organizations, including Rotary International. This group is best known for leading the way in eradicating polio from our planet, something Rotary International is proud to be a partner of in a world-wide effort that is almost accomplished. My lifestyle changes include being able to spend the summer visiting my extended family members in Finland, something we all look forward to with great anticipation. My life is more joyous than I ever thought possible.

It was not always like this. When I made the decision to change my life completely and start an online business during 2005, I had been teaching in the public schools in Los Angeles for almost 20 years. I've taught every grade level, from kindergarten through high school, as well as some adult school classes. Teaching was my passion for many years, but times changed and it became a job. After battling cancer and a serious work injury I decided it was time for me to move on.

At the same time I was teaching I also worked in real estate part-time. After school, on the weekends, and during vacations from the classroom, I listed properties, showed homes to potential buyers, and worked as a residential appraiser. The real estate world did not know that I also worked as a classroom teacher and vice versa. To say I was exhausted after a day at work is an understatement.

During 2005 I began to explore the possibilities for what I could do to replace my current income. At that time I lived in the San Fernando Valley of Los Angeles, and my bills included my house payment, car payment, and a variety of other expenses. My savings were extremely limited, so it wasn't like I could stop working and explore my next career. Instead, I needed to find something that would fit into my present lifestyle so I could learn a little at a time.

I turned my car into a rolling classroom, listening to CDs while driving to and from work. This was the most economical use of my time, and I purchased materials from several places to learn what was available to someone like me at this stage of my life. I had turned 50 that summer and thought that not as many doors would be open to me when it came to starting a new career at that point, in comparison if I were much younger. This was a limiting belief, but I believed it to be true at the time.

I listened to people like Brian Tracy and Bob Proctor and learned that my future was truly unlimited. This was great, but I still had no direction. Finally, I listened to a series of audios that discussed setting up a business on the Internet from your home computer. Now that got my attention!

I listened to this information again that weekend, but this time I did it from home where I could take copious notes and write down every website and reference that was mentioned. I could not believe what I was hearing. I had been using computers for my lessons in the classroom, my real estate business, and for personal reasons like research and email, yet I was unaware that people had been starting small businesses with little more than a home computer since the mid 1990s, and that were actually making a significant income.

It sounded like some type of parallel universe, and I wanted to know more.

Within a few weeks I was working on this several hours each week. Very quickly I realized that it would take me forever working at this pace. There was so much to learn and put into place. That's when I made the decision to resign from my teaching position in order to do this full time. I was able to cash out my retirement savings in order to have money to live on. At the same time I began giving away my best real estate clients to colleagues who were working in real estate on a full time basis.

I was burning the ships.

This was both frightening and exhilarating, but my decision had been made.

Those first few months were enlightening, as I slowly came to the realization that I knew nothing whatsoever about being an entrepreneur.

As a teacher I had been an employee and in my real estate business I owned a job.

Transforming myself into an entrepreneur was not going to be easy, but Brian Tracy had said that all of these were "learnable skills" and I believed him.

I started 10 blogs on a variety of topics ranging from small dog tips to health and fitness to reinventing your life. I started writing articles on every topic I could think of. My goal was to write several e-books quickly, so I just kept writing. I had always wanted to be a writer but had been told that my writing was not good enough. On the Internet there was no one to judge you in this regard, so I became a writer. After a few months I had lots of articles and blog posts, but had not made any money.

I was missing some crucial pieces of the puzzle, and I am going to share those with you here.

The first strategy I wish I had known about: Lists

The first thing I wish I had known is that you must start building a list right away. A list, in this context, refers to the prospects and clients you are attracting into your business. This is a coveted asset in the offline world as well as on the Internet.

The reason I didn't build my list at all during my first year online, and the reason most people still don't do this when they are just getting started, is that we all want to have everything set up as perfectly as possible before we open the doors and invite the world to see what we are doing as we build our business.

Let me say this another way: *Perfection has no place in your life as an entrepreneur. Strive for excellence instead.*

All of the blogs I was setting up should have had an opt-in box offering a free giveaway from the very beginning. Instead, every bit of the traffic and visitors I was sending to those sites with my keyword rich titles and through my article submissions all disappeared as quickly as it arrived.

If I had captured the names and email addresses of each person who stopped by to see what I was writing about, I would have been able to communicate with them on an ongoing basis as long as they stayed subscribed to my list.

As I continued to learn and improve my marketing I would have been able to convert many of them into buyers. By trying to make each site perfect, I missed a great opportunity to start building a valuable asset for my business – my subscriber's list.

Action Step #1: Make it easy to participate

Take a look at any site you have online, whether it is a blog or other type of site. Make sure that you have an opt-in box in the upper right-hand corner of the page so that visitors can see where to sign up immediately.

Persuading people to sign up is not quite as easy as it was in the past, so make sure you have something of value to offer them in exchange for their name and email address. I typically prepare a short report, about five to seven pages in length, and give it an appealing title. You want your prospect to feel as though they absolutely must have your free giveaway in order to find out the information you are sharing.

Finally I learned how to add these opt-in boxes to my sites (on a Wordpress site it's done by pasting the code generated from your auto responder service into a text widget in your sidebar), and then I moved on to a more advanced strategy of using opt-in pages in addition to my current sites. An opt-in page is a web page that has its own domain and tells a little about you and what you are offering in exchange for the name and email address of your prospect. These pages are extremely effective because the visitor has only two choices; stay on the page and opt in or leave the page altogether. I now have about 50 of these that cover just about every area of what I teach and what I promote as an affiliate marketer.

I started to make some money in 2007 through sales of my own products and affiliate products I was recommending to my small list. There was no one around to teach me exactly what to do, so I had to figure it all out for myself. Social media was in its infancy, so forums were really the only place to ask questions. It seemed like everyone in the forums had been online longer and was so much more knowledgeable that myself, so I tended to stay in the background and learn more from reading other people's comments and questions than from asking my own. This was all due to my lack of confidence, so I have no one to blame except for myself.

The second strategy I wish I had known about:
Learning and networking at conferences

I knew that there were live marketing events being held regularly around the country, and I longed to attend one and connect with other people who understood what it was that I was working to accomplish on the Internet with my business. The only thing stopping me was a lack of funds, so it wasn't until the spring of 2008 that I was able to attend my first Internet marketing conference. One of my friends gave me some frequent flyer miles so I could get my airline ticket from Los Angeles to Atlanta and back, and I found someone to share the hotel room with so that cost could be minimized. I was on my way.

Attending live events is such a crucial part of building a profitable business that it should be required of all new entrepreneurs. While I was teaching and working in real estate I attended conferences and seminars every year as a part of my continuing education requirements. When we come online it seems like an option, but it shouldn't be.

From the moment I arrived at the hotel in Atlanta for that first event, I knew I was in the right place. It was three full days of learning and networking. I met people there that I still know today. Some of them are now my students and customers and others have gone on to create their own online success stories.

That weekend gave me the confidence and the courage I needed to carry on and to move on to the next level in my business. I returned home with a new sense of understanding about what it means to be an entrepreneur and to have the power and the ability to forge ahead and chart your own course. I began creating more products and handling my business in a way that would ensure greater success in the coming months. I also vowed to attend another event before the end of 2008. I ended up attending two more events before that year was over.

Another thing happened to me while I was at the event in Atlanta. Not only did I have more self-confidence and a belief in what I could achieve now that I had more direction, I also realized that I could learn to become a speaker and present my information to others at events similar to this one. This led to a series of events in my own life that made me want to change what I was doing in other ways. My Rotary Club allowed me to start speaking to them, and soon I was invited to speak to our entire district. By the spring of 2009 I had been invited to speak at an Internet marketing event for the first time ever. My life was truly changing and it felt fantastic!

Action Step #2: Commit to an event
Find out which events will be held in your field of interest during the next six months and choose one to attend. These days there are events held across the United States, as well as in Europe, Australia, and Asia.

The best way to find out what's available is to join the lists of the people who are leaders within your particular niche, and to connect on the social media sites with them as well. This way you will find out what's going on well in advance and be able to work around your schedule so you can attend. I promise you that this will be worth it in a multitude of ways.

I don't know you personally, so I can only make a generalization when I say that most people who want to learn more about online business, seem to be looking for more than just a way to earn some extra money or to replace their current income entirely. After being online about five years at this point, it is my belief that new online entrepreneurs are also looking for more meaning in their lives. This was certainly the way I felt when I walked away from a teaching career that no longer fulfilled me and a thriving real estate business that was wearing me down physically.

I wanted a life that was more about doing the things I had always wanted to do in my life. This included being able to travel anytime I wanted to, getting involved with charitable causes I believed in, and becoming a published author.

The third strategy I wish I had known about:
It is never too late to change

The third thing I wish I had known from the very beginning is that we really can achieve anything we want in our lives. I lacked self-confidence when I was new and thought that no one would be interested in my perspective or point of view. If your current belief is that you don't have anything special or unique to offer to others, you must start turning your thinking around right away.

My mother used to tell me that I could do anything I wanted to in my life, but I did not believe her. I thought mothers had to say that kind of thing to their children to make them feel better about themselves. I was 50 years old by the time I figured out that she was right, and I'm just thankful she lived long enough to see some of the success I was able to achieve in both my personal and professional life.

Because we are all pioneers on the Internet, we can do whatever feels right for us. When I create a new product or a new course no one is there to tell me that it isn't what I should be doing with my time and efforts. My list and the marketplace guide me as to what is right at any particular point in time. This is the exact opposite of what we experience at a job.

A job requires you to follow a specific set of actions, leading to established company goals that may or may not reflect your personal feelings and beliefs. When I look back at the twenty years I spent teaching for the public school system I wonder why I didn't speak up more often and how I lasted so long in that restrictive environment.

Anything we make up our mind to do is definitely doable, so think about what the ideal business would look like to you. I have found that I am more productive now than at any time in my life previously, and it is due to the fact that live each day according to what works best for me. This is completely subjective because all of us are unique individuals with different abilities and desires.

Action step # 3: Plan your day

Write down what you would like to achieve by having an online business. If this will be intended as supplemental income, at least for now, write that down. If your goal is to replace your current income or an income that was lost due to being downsized or laid off, write that down.

Now write a few paragraphs about what your ideal day would look like. Ask yourself some pointed questions, such as:

- What time would you arise each morning?

- Who would be at your house?
- What would you eat for breakfast?
- When would your workday begin?
- What would you be doing as part of that work?
- Who would you be serving?
-

It was when I first did this that I realized I'm not a "morning person" after all. Even though I spent the better part of 20 years getting up before 5 am, five days a week, and leaving my house before 6 o'clock in order to beat the traffic and arrive at work early enough to get a jump on my day. It was not a schedule that made me happy. I longed to stay home during the day and enjoy my home and surroundings. Now I am able to do that anytime I like.

I mentioned that I had always wanted to write but had been discouraged early on. Now I write every day, typically in the mornings after I let my dogs out and prepare a light breakfast. This suits my personality and makes me feel productive and alive. I've written five books so far and love this part of my life.

Working from home on your computer, or from wherever you happen to be that has an Internet connection, is a way of life that was unknown to previous generations. This has changed the face of entrepreneurship forever. If this is something you feel compelled to pursue then you must jump in right away and get started. I hope you have benefitted from the three strategies I have shared with you here. I would love to hear how this has impacted your life and what else you need in order to achieve your goals and dreams. Sharing ideas and strategies and serving you in this regard in part of my life's work. You can do anything you set your mind to, and it all begins with the first step.

Editors' note

Connie is an inspiration to us all. A cancer survivor, Connie shows us how perseverance, belief in yourself, and the willingness to work hard really CAN move mountains - if you have a game plan.

Life is a classroom. Wherever you go, there are opportunities for learning - if only we are both willing and open to listen. Whether you find a mentor, as some of our expert authors have suggested, or turn your car into a "rolling classroom" as Connie did, doing your homework and educating yourself is key. Not only do you not know some things, you also "don't know what you don't know." And that ignorance can be costly when starting a business.

Connie's example provides hope for so many people who are faced with such incredible career challenges in this economy: teachers being laid off. Military men and women returning home from service. So many who have incredible transferable skills that they might not even realize they have - and can be applied in a web-based business. Coupled with the translatable skills you have - realizing that the rest is all learnable skills - could set you free.

In building your business online, don't forget that people still do business with other people - not 'companies' or logos. Work on developing a customer base (list) just as you would in traditional business. Meet your customers and really talk with them (social media, participation) just as you would in a storefront. Get out there and get to know others in your industry (conferences) just as a local business owner might go to the Chamber of Commerce meetings or attend industry tradeshows.

All of this advice from Connie, as well as many of our other expert authors, often means that we have to change - how we think about business, how we think about money or products - and very often how we think about ourselves. And change - especially at that very personal level is scary stuff for us all, at times.

Entrepreneurial life is messy. It's ok to be afraid - just as all of our expert authors have been afraid at different points in time in their careers. Just don't let that fear of change or failure or imperfection paralyzes you. In a Main street store front things are not perfect - and neither will your web-based storefront. Dishes fall and break; things get misplaced; there are holes in the system from time to time. Don't let the idea that "everything lives forever on the web" intimidate you. Every ONE of the authors have made mistakes - but that means you can learn from their mistakes - you don't have to make the same mistakes they did.

For more information about this author, or to learn more about how to start your own web-based business, go to www.mcmoodycrawford.com. There you can also sign up for our newsletter and announcements about our upcoming events.

..

ABOUT JANE MARK

Jane Mark is a pocket dynamo who has a typical New York attitude. "Don't tell me how hard it is or how much effort it will take, get it done."

Jane has extensive knowledge of the business world. She ran a multi-million dollar real estate partnership called JED Management Corp. She started her own successful catering business in the heart of New York City's Central Park, which was named — you guessed it – "Jane's." She has extensive knowledge of people's needs and behavior patterns having received her masters in psychology from the New School for Social Research in New York and a BA from Brandeis University in Massachusetts. This training and her extensive business background have given Jane a unique perspective into both doing business on the Internet and discovering what people want by asking the right kinds of questions.

Jane is the author of four successful e-books, All Your Lists In One Place, Joe? Yes Mable Are We Rich Yet?, The Magic Bullet, and the definitive Guide to Sokule – Sokule – It's Not Your Grandmother's Social Media Site. Jane takes care of Joint Venture Partnerships and marketing. She writes the creative ads that give the business its zing!

You will often find her on the phone with clients offering marketing tips or delving into the support desk to give a personal touch to Client queries. She is all hands on deck all the time. To Jane every client, large or small, is treated as a VIP.

Jane is the partner of the website developer, Phil Basten. Phil has developed such well-known sites as Sokule and KuleSearch, social media aggregators and search engine aggregators that let businesses reach millions of potential customers with just 1 click.

6

IF ONLY...

by JANE MARK
www.sokule.com

I try to avoid words like this whenever I can.

If you keep them around they can cause great anxiety in your personal life, in your job, or in your business.

If you dwell on "if only's", you may find yourself paralyzed and unable to move in one direction or another, or unable to make decisions that are important in your life or your business.

There is, of course, something you can do about this phenomenon... If you experience an "if only" moment in your life, learn from it.

When you step back from the hustle and bustle of everyday life, and you review and learn from the past, you will have begun the journey to a more perfect future.

I'm Jane Mark. I'm a mother, a grandmother, and a businesswoman. I'm a wife, a musician, and a storyteller. I'm the President of Sokule Inc., and you will find me hanging out with many of my online friends at www.sokule.com .

Online, I am known as the "Queen of Lists." But, I am also a Social Media developer and expert. I am the author of several books, the latest being: Sokule: This is not your Grandmother's Social Media Site.

I love to goof around and have fun. Phil Basten, my Australian partner and I, created two zany online characters called Joe and Mable based on a book we wrote called – "Joe? Yes Mable? Are We Rich Yet?"

We turned the book into a 1940s radio show that we called the Joe and Mable Show you can listen to at http://joeandmable.com .

When I was asked to write a chapter for this first book in a planned series on Internet marketing, sales and business, I jumped at the chance. This was right up my alley and I knew that I had a few "if only's" in my closet I could share that might just help a few people avoid them.

The future no doubt holds more "if only" moments, and many more things I wish I had known, but right now, here are the ones that are important.

I have a very simple philosophy. When you stop learning, you stop breathing. Since I would like to continue breathing for many years to come here are some lessons I learned.

I have broken this down in to three parts to simplify it and make it easier to follow.
- Part 1 - The Partner from Hell
- Part 2 - Outsource to success
- Part 3 - How to be profitable from day one

Without parts 1 and 2, Phil and I would not have reached part 3 so let us begin our journey.

The "partner from Hell"...
Try to picture this:
- You are around 50 years old.
- You live in Australia.
- You lose your job and you spend many months looking for employment.
- You used to be able to walk into any job your wanted.
- Now you can't even get to first base.
- Everyone turns you down.

If you are over 45 in Australia, no one wants to hire you. You are over the hill and obsolete. This happened to my partner Phil.

It was summer, 1998 and Phil was faced with a choice. He could hire himself or starve. He hired himself.

Back in those days Phil had little knowledge of the computer. He had an old 386 clunker of a computer at home that worked something like a 100 car freight train going through a busy crossing.

Phil was determined not to let this beast get the better of him. He turned it on, fought with it, cursed it, and eventually got it to bend to his will.

He then spent an entire year browsing around the Net, looking at what people were doing to make money online. He figured the Internet was the new employment center of the decade and he'd better master it fast.

Phil saw that safe lists were becoming increasingly popular mainly due to spammers, and that both marketers and business people needed a safe environment to tell others about their services.

But he also noticed that the ones that made money were those who hosted the safe lists and got paid every month for hosting them. Another thing he saw was that many of these lists were individual lists that had to be setup separately.

This was too cumbersome and messy for Phil. So, he created the framework for the Internet's first fully integrated safe list hosting script that made it extremely easy to setup and sell access to these lists on the Internet.

But there was a problem. Phil knew nothing about PHP programming. Now he needed someone to program the script. He also had no money to invest. Unemployment has a nasty habit of depleting your resources.

Enter the partner from Hell
So Phil put the word out that he was looking for a programmer to work on a 50/50 partnership basis, where the programmer would contribute the programming skill and Phil would contribute the marketing content.

A young kid answered the call. Like Phil he had no money either but he had talent and Phil that if they teamed up they could do something cool together. After much back and forth the product was finally ready for prime time and the sales started flowing in. They split the income and both were earning a decent income.

But Phil wanted to grow even bigger, so came up with the concept for the Internet's first automatic safe-list submitter. Again Phil's young partner did the programming. It was also a success and more money came in monthly. These were not huge sums, but they were consistent, and it sure beat being unemployed.

One day Phil noticed that the lists he had being building for more than a year were growing smaller not bigger. He noticed that people were disappearing like water in a dessert. The income began to dwindle and the monthly records he kept on the business grew smaller and smaller.

It became apparent that the programmer had been removing people from their joint lists and moving them somewhere else to a cloned copy of the script, so that when Phil tried to sell a solo ad service to his lists, he could no longer mail to many of them. They were gone.

Phil confronted his partner. Where are the people? Where did you bury them?

The answer he got back was "Look old man. You are never going to amount to anything. You have no talent. I have the codes for the lists and for the submitter and I have the only access to the servers and I am cutting you off."

Phil could not access the lists. The monthly income from the submitter stopped.

So once again Phil was unemployed. Again he was face with a choice. Sue the kid, or walk away and start again. He chose to walk.

Eventually the programmer faded into oblivion and Phil went on to develop some of the most successful advertising sites on the Net.

The programmer had talent but Phil had something even more important. He had knowledge of what people wanted and what they were willing to pay money for and, he knew how to sell it to them.

The moral of the story…

Choose your partners wisely. Put everything in writing. If you are the developer and you work with a programmer, make sure you have access to all of the coding and the servers at all times.

If possible don't partner with the programmer unless you know them well or you know someone who has used them and recommends them. You are in a much stronger position with programmers if you are paying them for their work not partnering with them.

If after many projects together you feel it is a good idea to partner with the programmer, make sure you take steps to protect yourself. Phil now uses many different programmers in many different countries and partners with none of them.

But partners from hell do not just come in the form of programmers or young kids. Even if you get something in writing from a partner, they may not follow through on the deal and you are left in the lurch with nothing to show for your efforts.

I do a lot of joint venture, or JV, deals with people on the Net. They always follow a certain pattern. I promote for the JV partner if the site is compatible with the needs of my lists and the partner provides a Sokule Bonus to their paid members that is visible at their site.

It is a formula that works for both sides. They get the strength of my promotions. I get visibility for our main site, Sokule. Usually I check to see that the Sokule bonus is showing and available before I promote for someone.

Recently, I took a program under my wing and promoted the heck out of it. I was high up on the leader's board but the site was in prelaunch so no actual paid members existed. When the site launched and people began paying, I wondered why there was no one requesting the Sokule bonus.

Much to my surprise there was no Sokule bonus in sight. They had not put it up anywhere. When I contacted them about this, I got a BS story that was not worth listening to. I immediately cancelled my account and insisted that my name and profile be taken off the leader's board. But it was too late. They had my list subscribers. I had inadvertently misrepresented to my list subscribers that I had been given a top position in this company, which as it turns out, I did not receive as promised.

So even though I have my own careful rules about whom I partner with, and even though I get things in writing, I still get burned from time to time.
So I quickly learned to check everything before I start promoting for anyone.

Phil and I wish we had known these things when we first started out. It could have saved us a lot of frustration and anxiety.

Outsource to success...

About three years ago I was at a JV Alert Conference in Washington DC. Phil and I put ourselves on the "hot seat:" a venue where you present a problem to a panel of experts and you get their input so you can solve it.

This was the problem: Phil and I had grown our business to a seven-figure business over a period of about 5 years. But we were stuck in neutral. The business was neither growing nor shrinking.

While a seven-figure income is nothing to sneeze at, Phil and I look at business as a challenge and we are always looking for ways to grow it and reach new heights.

So there we were on the hot seat. One of the experts, Stephanie Frank, simply said, "You can't get from 1 million to 5 million with what you are doing now. You need to change it. You need to get some help."

Now, I should mention that people had been saying that to us for years, and I had always resisted. We do have some help, of course. We have a team of programmers who work with us and our sites,, but until about two years ago Phil had always handled all of the development aspects of the business and I handled all the support, finances, sales promotions, and JV partner development.

We were a two-person show and it was taking a toll on both of us.

When Stephanie said: "You can't get from 1 million to 5 million the way you are going," I knew she was right. So off we went to outsource some of our more routine work. The head of the programming company we were working with offered support help and we took him up on it.

Last year I met Daven Michaels from 123employee and we hired one of his staff to do our entire posting on Sokule, to write some of our articles and to post our videos through Traffic Geyser and Pingler.

The simple addition of just those two people took an enormous burden off our backs and we saw our revenue increase as soon as we brought this help onboard.

So the lesson we learned: Outsource what you can if you want to grow your way to success. Sometimes it is hard to let go of the things that you do every day in your business. You have your own way of doing them and you know they get done right.

The problem is, time is limited and there is only so much you can do alone. If you try to do it all yourself, then you may find you have little time left to think and to be creative and to take care of the things that really grow your business.

I wish I had known this when I first started out. My business may have been double or triple the size it is now.

My support people are great at what they do, but they will never do things the way I do them, and I don't expect them too.

My sites are my babies. No one does things quite like me. But when you hand over your work to someone else, the benefits far outweigh the small losses in "perfection."

There are some things, however, that you cannot outsource: company finances, for example. Sure we have accountants but I am talking about day-to-day access to our PayPal, AlertPay, and our bank accounts.

I have heard too many horror tales about outsourcing your finances to let that happen to us. If you have someone in your family who you absolutely trust with your life, then perhaps you can outsource your financial dealings. Short of that be very careful who you give access to your finances to.

I can still hear Stephanie now in my sleep. "Jane, you will never get from 5 million to 10 million like that." Perhaps she is right :-) We will see.

How to make a website profitable from Day One
So far we have covered how important it is to pick the right JV partner when you start out in business, or even when your business is mature. We have showed you how important it is to outsource some of the more routine elements of your business so you can focus on growing it.

Now it is time to talk money: The green spending stuff everyone wants to get his or her hands on quickly.

The approach that I am about to describe now is not for everyone.

When Phil and I tried this, we had been on the Net for nine years. We had large lists. Our members knew who we were and they trusted us.

It was May 2009 and Phil and I set off on one of our biggest adventures to date, the development and financing of our site called Sokule, http://sokule.com

To begin with we were looking to develop a way around email.

One day we stumbled upon Twitter and we thought this is a great platform but it is not built for business. So we modeled Sokule after Twitter, but monetized and set it up so that would be similar to Twitter, but for business.

We also wanted Sokule to be uniquely different.

When Sokule was just a gleam in Phil's eye, we sat down with some Twitter experts, Ron Davies, Susan and David Preston, and Willie Crawford, at a JV Alert Conference and told them what we were up to.

They loved the idea and shared their thoughts with us.

We decided early on that this was going to take a good deal of money to get this project moving and that we did not want to take it out of our existing business. So we began to formulate a plan to fund this from day one.

When you go to finance a business, conventional wisdom tells you that you have basically four choices.
1.   You can try to get a loan from a bank.
2.   You can max your credit card or your bank account.
3.   You can hit the old folks up - Ask Dad or Mom.
4.   You can take on an angel investor.

We weren't happy with any of those choices. So we went to our members and said:

Guys and Gals:
We have a great idea. We can't tell you much about it but you will love it. We can tell you that whatever we do at this site, you will get absolutely everything we offer when we launch and you will get whatever we add in the future absolutely free.

We can tell you this much…
•   It will be an advertising site.
•   You will be able to get your own business noticed fast and easily
•   You will be able to do JV's with Phil and I.

- You will get advance notice of every site we ever launch in the future so you can let your people know about it first and,
- You will be able to make 50% commissions on all sales that you make at the site.

We also told them. We don't have a website yet.

When you think about it, we didn't give them a whole lot to go on.

We told them we were going to charge them a one-time fee of $1299 for a founder membership and we let them know that these memberships would be strictly limited at this price.

No sooner did we put the word out about this up and coming website, the money began to pour in. In the space of 30 days, we had sold 125 founding memberships or over $162,000 before we opened the doors or had a website online.

Our opening expenses were about $75,000, which consisted of programming costs, server costs, and advertising costs.

So before we had a website online we had secured a net profit of $87,000.

When we opened up the site a few months later and people saw the actual site, they loved it, and 60 days later we had sold another 400 founding memberships That added an additional half million dollars to our bottom line.

Many other memberships ranging from $9.95/month to $197/annual were sold too, but when the doors opened, it was the founding memberships that people gobbled up in droves. Over the course of the next 12 months, almost all of the 1500 initial release founding memberships had been purchased.

The price went up to $1795 and is currently at $2495. We are holding on to about 100 spaces in reserve for future promotions.

Shortly after we instituted this 'client-based investment as a financing model,' sites all over the Net started announcing founding memberships. We had hit on a model that others wanted to copy. Sokule was profitable from day one.

Now: There are a few caveats.

If you are new to the Net and don't have a list, or at least a history of delivering good products to your clients, this method of financing your project will be very difficult to pull off.

The reason we were able to pre-sell our products to our list members is because they knew us and knew that when we said we would deliver a good site, they could take that to the bank.

In the 12 years we have been online, we have launched more than 60 sites. None were as successful as Sokule, but all were profitable. We have never closed a site that we launched, and we have never had a site that was a complete failure.

If you are a newcomer to the Internet and you do not have a list or a track record of success and you do not have the money to finance your ideas yourself, there are still a number of ways you can start building and growing your business:

- You can start as an affiliate and earn the money you need to finance your project.
- You can look for JV partners who can help you get started.
- You could find a programmer you can work with long term.
- You can find a website designer who has some good copy writing talent and form an alliance with them.

But before you do any of these, make sure they are NOT "The Partners from Hell."

If you are passionate and have fun in your business, it will prosper.

Editors' note

Jane Mark brings to life a common challenge we all face - the idea even this book would founded on... "If only I knew then..." Hindsight is always 20/20 as several of the expert authors have attested to. The key is to not get trapped in that reflective, wishful thinking. While there are no mulligans (do-overs) in real life - you can keep from making the same mistakes a second time... or in this case learning from others so you don't have to make the same mistakes at all.

So often our society gets so caught up in the celebrations of who we are as successful people that we forget that sometimes there were years of utter, dismal failure. There were gut wrenching hard times. These times were painful - and as human beings - even those who are successful - no one wants to think about painful times like the ones Jane shares with us here.

But Jane brings to light two major points: you don't get the successful, happy times without usually having the bad stuff too; and you can learn from those bad times. In fact - ask any entrepreneur what their biggest learning moments were - and more often than not they will share with you a painful experience.

Pain is a part of life. We like to avoid it. We can't. But we can learn from it, just as Jane and Phil have, and grow into more than we ever thought possible.

Jane also points out that, just as several other expert authors have shared; life and business are "long games." For those who are trapped in the "Internet Lottery" idea that money comes fast, all too often they are trading temporary money and success for long term real wealth, security and happiness. By capitalizing on your real skills, by focusing on who you are, what you want your business to be and shaping it around those core elements, you too can be a winner at the long game.

For more information about this author, or to learn more about how to start your own web-based business, go to www.mcmoodycrawford.com. There you can also sign up for our newsletter and announcements about our upcoming events.

ABOUT SUSANNE MYERS

Sweet, smart, and slick-as-snot, Susanne Myers is a little powerhouse with a huge affiliate marketing presence but don't let her quiet demeanor fool you. Susanne's brain works at the speed of light formulating plans and plotting to take over whatever niche she happens to be working on at the time.

When Susanne was pregnant with her daughter she started researching the whole "making money online" gig and finally decided to jump in full-tilt-boogie about 7 years ago.

Today, both Susanne and her husband are full-time affiliate marketers and true entrepreneurs at heart. In fact, her beautiful 3rd Grade daughter has her very own affiliate blogs and makes money following the advice of her mother. The journey to a 6-figure income was filled with twists, turns and yes, failure but Susanne never let the mistakes get her down. She educated herself and quickly learned how to choose profitable niche markets and the rest, as they say, is history.

Today, Susanne has taken her love of all things Internet and affiliate marketing and has started to teach others how to claim the same success she's found by using a step-by-step, this-is-exactly-how-I-did-it strategy.

You can find Susanne sharing her insights on various webinars, her own site, Twitter and Facebook and if you're really lucky you can hear her in person at several live events throughout the year.

7

COMMUNICATIONS IS YOUR LINK TO SUCCESS

by SUSANNE MYERS
www.AffiliateTreasurechest.com

You've heard of 20/20 hindsight, haven't you?

Today, I want to share three pieces of advice with you on things I could have done different or better when I first set out to make money online. Just like the examples my colleagues are sharing with you in this book, I hope you will learn from my past mistakes and get off to a better start with your Internet Business.

You may be tempted to dismiss some of the things we are sharing: please don't. There's no reason for you to cross some of the hurdles we've crossed. There's no reason for you to waste time, money and effort on things that just don't work. There's no reason for you to make some of the mistakes we've made or experience some of the serious setbacks we've come back from.

In this section, I would like to share some of the things I wish I'd done differently. When I was asked to contribute a chapter to this edition, I sat down and made a list of some of the mistakes I've made over the past seven years. I ended up with a list of over 30 things I could have shared with you today (and it was actually quite depressing to see all of them listed in black and white). I picked the three that made the biggest difference to my online business once I corrected them.

Before we get started, one quick piece of advice: While we put this book together so you won't make some of the mistakes we've made, don't ever be afraid to make your own.

Even after taking every single piece of advice in this book to heart, you will still make mistakes of your own. You'll mess up and some of your ventures are bound to fail. Don't worry about it... learn from it and move on. That's what we did and it's a big reason why we are successful when many others aren't.

Don't be afraid to fail... fail a lot. Try things and find what works for you. The faster you fail, the faster you'll be able to create a full-time income with your online business.

'Built it and they will come' just doesn't work

It took me about six months to learn this lesson the hard way. The year was 2004 and I was a young mom desperate to figure out a way to do this Internet stuff and make enough money to be able to stay home with my 1-year old. Since parenting was on my mind a lot, I started building a parenting website with lot so fun crafts and recipes along with all sorts of parenting advice articles.

This was long before I'd ever heard of WordPress or any other type of CMS (Content Management System), which means I was building my site the hard way... first by hand, coding html in notepad documents, then with Microsoft FrontPage.

Each new page, each new piece of content took a lot of time to add and that was all I did. I figured if I just kept adding content and made my site bigger and prettier, it would have to succeed, right?

Very wrong... the little part I forgot about was that you couldn't just build a site and then expect people to magically find it. Build it and they will come might work with certain baseball fields, but it doesn't with your websites.
It's like building a store out in the middle of nowhere without any roads leading to it and no advertisement for it anywhere. No matter how big your store is and how pretty the sign out front is... no one is going to find it if they don't know about it.

The same holds true for your Internet business and your website(s). You have to go out there and tell the world about them. You have to market, advertise, and build links to it so your target market can find you.

I slowly started spending some time marketing my site, not nearly enough in the beginning, but every little bit helped. If your site is still fairly new and you need to spend a good bit of time adding more content to it, aim to spend 50% of your time working on your site and 50% out there marketing it. (More on that in a second...)

Ideally though, you want to spend about 20% of your time on your site and 80% marketing it ... shoot for that as your end goal. Anytime I remind myself of this rule and put it to good use my traffic goes up, my lists grow faster and my income increases.

Let me give you some ideas on different things I'm doing right now to market my sites. Pick just two or three of them to begin with and start using them. As you start seeing results and get more comfortable with each, come back to this section and add another one to your online marketing arsenal.

Blog commenting

When I first started building website, there were no blogs (or at least I wasn't aware of any). The web has changed quite a bit over the past few years and I now use blog commenting quite a bit to give new sites a boost to start spreading the word about them.

When I launched my affiliate marketing blog a little over two years ago at www.AffiliateTreasureChest.com, I spent quite a bit of time commenting on other blogs. I saw a nice spike in traffic and fairly big names in our Industry started mentioning me on social media sites like Twitter and Facebook and linked to posts on my blog in their own blog posts. Traffic was steadily climbing up and my readership started growing.

A few months into this I got sidetracked with other projects and stopped commenting on blogs all together. I also slowed down my own blogging. It didn't take long for traffic on my site to slow down to a trickle. Thankfully I was able to pick things back up, but it was slow going. Had I continued to comment more regularly, I'm sure my blog would be much more widely read right now and who knows what other doors may have opened.

If you're already blogging, this will be an easy way to get started. Find three to five big blogs in your niche. Chances are you already know what these blogs are. You can also find them by doing a search on Technorati.com or via Google Blog Search.

Once you have your list of blogs, visit them once a day and leave a meaningful comment. Link back to your own site via the URL field in the comment submission form. I recommend using your name (or the pen name you're using for your site) in the name field.

Don't link back to your own site within the comment itself and don't just spam the comment section. Put some thought into your writing and add to the conversation. If people like what you have to say, they will click on the link on your name and come to your own website or blog.

Forum posting

Forums are another way I use to reach potential readers of my blogs. And I have to admit it isn't something I do as regularly as I should. Whenever I do set aside some time to participate on a handful of good affiliate marketing forums, I see some very positive results.

After getting back from an Internet Marketing Conference (NAMS) a few weeks ago, I started actively posting on a forum set up for conference participants. I also started spending a little time on Lynn Terry's forum at www.Clicknewz.com and poked my head into the Warrior Forum a little. Within a couple of days, traffic to my affiliate marketing blog nearly doubled and I had 30 new readers sign up for my list.

Ready to give it a try? Find two or three active forums in your niche. Set up a profile on each and be sure to include a link back to your site. If the forum allows it, set up a signature file with your name and a link back to your site.
Post a few times per week on each forum. Answer questions and start a few interesting threads of your own. Again, it's important to focus on quality here and add to the conversation.

Social media

Apparently the story of my life is coming late to the game... but the good news is that it doesn't matter. Better to start late than never. I didn't really get social media for a couple of years. I set up some profiles and would chat with my friends on occasion, but that was about it.

That's until I started looking at an account I had set up for one of my bigger niche sites. I totally forgot about it, and had not logged into it for a few months. I had page after page of friend requests, but more amazingly, people were talking about the site and to each other. They were sharing links to content within my site, making recommendations and the likes.

Even without my involvement, they were using my Facebook profile as a hub to meet and exchange ideas. I've since hired someone to monitor that profile and had her set up a dedicated Facebook page. Facebook is now the 4th largest traffic referrer to the site.

I don't even want to think about how much traffic I could be getting from Facebook on a regular basis, had I become active a long time ago (not to mention the other big social media sites).

My recommendation? Set up a Twitter, Facebook, and Google Plus account. If there are other social networks for your niche, you may want to become active there as well. (For example, LinkedIn works well for business owners).

Include a link back to your site within the profile pages of each of your accounts. Then start to make friends. Talk to people in your target market via these social media sites. Ask them questions, start conversations.

On occasion, link back to interesting content on your website or blog. Don't try to sell social media sites. Build relationships and develop your readership.

Social bookmarking

Here's my story about social bookmarking. I remember when these sites first started popping up. I'm always been "a-one-laptop-kinda-gal." I could see the benefit of having a list of bookmarks online if you were using multiple computers, but for me, the one built into the browser worked just fine, thank-you-very-much.

Then I looked at some of my traffic stats (I use Google Analytics) and noticed that I was getting a LOT of traffic to several of my niche sites from Stumbleupon. I realized that people weren't just using these bookmarks from multiple computers; they were compiling topic-specific lists of pages they loved and then shared them with their friends. I was hooked. I did some research into plugins that would make it easier for my readers to bookmark pages on my sites and I spent some time bookmarking myself and building relationships with others on these sites.

It's a little hard to measure the overall impact this has had on my traffic, but social bookmarking sites still shop up high on my list of referring sites, especially for sites in the homemaking and cooking niche.

Below you will find a list of a few good general social bookmarking sites. These will bring you quite a bit of traffic and are certainly worth submitting to. The sign up and submission process for each is pretty self-explanatory and you can find "how to" help at each of these sites.

Start by signing up for an account at each of these sites. I recommend you set up a separate email address for this to avoid bogging down your main email.

- Stumbleupon
- Reddit
- Digg
- Delicious
- Mixx
- Newsvine
- Diigo
- Propeller
- Mister Wong
- Faves
- Multiply

Next, start submitting your home page to all of these sites. Then work your way through submitting one to two sites per day to as many of these sites as you can. Spend a few minutes each day at each site (or at least a few of the sites) browsing through other submissions and voting / commenting on them.

Be sure to recommend some new sites you come across in your research as well.

If you are running your site on WordPress, I recommend you also use a plug-in like "Sociable" that allows your readers to bookmark content for you and share it via social media sites.

Article marketing

I've been using article marketing since the day I realized that I couldn't just keep building my website and expect people to show up out of nowhere. I started out writing articles for Ezinearticles.com. I've been a member there since April 19, 2005 (yes, I had to look that up. Thankfully they are better at keeping track of stuff like that than I am).

Since that day, my articles have been viewed 579,478 times and I've gotten 31,085 visits to my various websites... and that's from just one directory (Ezinearticles.com) and having written only 339 articles. Just imagine how much traffic I could be getting if I was as dedicated as my good friend Connie Ragen Green who writes at least one article per day.

Article marketing is another simple and free way to get exposure for your website. The idea is simple... Write a 400+ word informative article on a topic that's closely related to what your site is about. For example, if my website is about crock pot cooking, I may write about how to choose the perfect crock pot, how to care for my crock pot or how to adapt a recipe for crock pot cooking.

Write a resource box that invites readers back to your site. I like to include two links when possible ... one to my home page and the other to an individual article or blog post.

Submit your article to a few article directories. People will find them there, but the main purpose of these directories is to allow other webmasters to grab your content and publish it on their sites and in their ezines (or online newsletters).

Here are some article directories I like to use:
- Ezinearticles.com
- GoArticles.com
- Isnare.com
- LadyPens.com
- ArticleBase.com
- Buzzle.com
- IdeaMarketers.com

Get in the habit of writing and submitting a few articles per week and watch traffic to your site grow.

Guest blogging

Guest blogging is another rather recent online marketing strategy I started implementing. It grew out of my blog commenting efforts. When I spent a fair amount of time commenting on a particular blog and adding to the conversation, I would often get an email from the blogger with an invitation to share more with their readers. It has expanded my reach and audience quite a bit. I know get several emails per month from people that start with something along the lines of: "I came across your blog on Nicole Dean's site and love what you're doing. I was wondering if you could help me..."

Guest blogging allows me to connect with real people in my niche that have problems and questions that I can help you with and so can you.

Once you start building a relationship with some of the bloggers in your niche (by commenting on their blogs regularly), you can approach them about guest blogging. This simply means that you write a blog post for them that they can then publish.

Within the blog post, you can link back to your site. I recommend you also invite readers at the end of your post to visit your blog or website.

Why do you want to spend time writing for another site? Simple… it gives you the chance to get in front of an audience. The blogger in question has spent some time gaining traffic and building a reputation in your niche. Take advantage of that fact and get in front of that readership by writing guest blog posts.

A word of advice… Chances are that you'll write quite a few guest blog posts, email them to the blog owner and they don't end up getting published. Sometimes they will let you know that they won't be able to use it, but many times you're simply ignored. Don't let that discourage you.

You can either use the content you've written on your own blog, or offer it to another blogger. Above all, keep at it and keep approaching other bloggers about guest blogging opportunities. As your reputation in the market place grows and you're showing up on more and more blogs, it'll get easier.

Video marketing

Video marketing is something I'm just starting to work on. It's actually quite simple. You record a short, informational video and upload it to YouTube.com and other video sharing websites.

Did you know that YouTube is the second biggest search engine (right after Google)? I don't have enough experience right now to teach you much about video marketing, but wanted to mention it here as something else to look into and use to market your site.

Viral reports

Last but not least, let's talk about my personal favorite … creating viral reports. These are short 7 to 15 page long pdf documents that you can share in various ways. I use articles and blog posts I've written as the basis of my reports. Each report includes several links back to my website.

You can then use the report to grow your list (by offering it as a giveaway), spread it via social media sites and submit it to document-sharing sites like Scribd.com.

I also like to make some of my reports available for download on my blog. Within the report, invite readers to share it with others. That's what makes it viral and can cause it to be shared all over the Internet, introducing you to all sorts of new readers.

Take a look at some of my free reports here:
http://www.scribd.com/susanne_myers/documents

Back up everything!

Let me share my biggest nightmare story with you ... A few years ago I was running a membership site with a friend. It was doing quite well with several hundred paying members.

I woke up one morning, got my coffee and started going through emails....

I saw a quite a few emails from members who couldn't log in (which was strange) and then read one send by a friend who pointed out that our home page had all sorts of strange Arabic text on it along with a message letting us know that our website had been hijacked. They provided an email address to contact them about payment... they had hacked our website and wanted to get paid to restore it – YIKES!

Needless to say, I panicked. When I got back to my senses, I contacted our webhosting company. Scott did an awesome job figuring out what happened (there was a vulnerability in the membership site software we were using that we weren't aware of) and insured me that this wouldn't be a big deal. We'd just delete everything and then restore the site from last night's backup.

I went about my day, glad this was being taken care of. Or so I thought...

A few hours later Scott got back to me to let me know that the website backup from the night before had been corrupted by the hackers as well. Next he figured out that the hosting company's backup hadn't been set up correctly. Instead of saving multiple versions, each night the backup from the previous day was overwritten... and the backup for the backup failed...

To make a long story short, we lost about 6 months worth of data. I had most of the content we'd added during that time saved on my own computer, but we lost a lot of customer and subscriber data. All in all, it was about a $30,000 mistake.

It would have been easy to blame it on the hosting company, but really it was our mistake. This was our business and we should not have relied on just them to backup our various databases.

I hear stories on almost a weekly basis of online entrepreneurs losing content, subscribers, customers and all sorts of other data simply because they don't back up everything. Don't let that happen to you.

Here are some of the things that should be backed up (by you) regularly. I use several hard drives along with some online data storage services for this.
- Website Content
- Website Databases (like the one for your blog etc.)
- Emails
- Articles (don't just have them on Ezinearticles.com ... have a copy on your own computer as well).
- Videos (you heard about YouTube accounts being deleted, right?)
- Audio Recordings
- Webinar Recordings.
- Digital Products (including e-books, short reports etc.)

If you spend time, writing, recording or building something, you should have several backups for it.

It may also be a good idea to talk to your hosting company to see what type of backup they have in place. Don't rely on just them, but make sure they have a good process in place in addition to what you're doing.

If you're not sure how to back something up (a mySQL database for example), take the time to learn it this week or hire someone to take care of these backups for you.

Build your email list from day one
If I could go back in time and give my past self just one piece of advice, it would be to start building an email list much sooner. It was another one of those things I kept dragging my feet on because it seemed too complicated and it cost money to sign up with an auto responder service.

Truth is, it isn't very hard at all, and I now gladly pay my bill for AWeber (my auto responder of choice) because it makes me multiple times what I pay them.

I now have lists for most of my niche sites. Some are free subscribers, some are customer lists. On any given day, I can email well over 75,000 people because of these lists.

I'm able to send out weekly newsletter to get readers back to my websites and share good content on those sites. I'm profiting via affiliate offers, my own products and Google AdSense on some of those sites.

I also have a growing list of auto responder messages that go out to various lists. This means that as soon as a new person signs up, they start receiving a sequence of emails. Some of the messages are pure content (tips and ideas specific to a particular niche), while others are offers for affiliate products.

Last but not least, whenever I come across a good offer, or if I need a little extra cash for some unexpected bills, all I have to do is sit down and write an email to one of my lists. A few minutes later the sales notifications start pouring in.

Let me tell you, that's a nice security blanket to have!

Had I started building lists from day one though, I could easily have over 100,000 readers at this point and I would have been able to make a full-time income with this "Internet marketing" stuff sooner.

Do yourself a favor… go to susanne.aweber.com right now and sign up for the $1 trial. Set up your first list using the step-by-step wizard and help tutorials on their site. Then stick a sign up form on your site.

As you get more comfortable, start learning more about email marketing, different ways to send emails, making offers within those mailings etc.

Some other things to look into are:
- Creating an opt-in Page
- Split testing signup forms.
- Creating an "ethical bribe" to get more people to sign up.
- Sending more traffic to your opt-in page.
- Improving opt-in rates.
- Writing good subject lines
- Writing good email copy.
- Improving Open Rates

But here's the thing… you don't have to know all that stuff to start building your list. Start with the basics, get comfortable, get a few hundred people on your list and then start looking into everything else you can do.
For now, just do something – anything to start building your email list from day one!

Editors' note
Everyone lives with 20/20 hindsight. As you've now started to gather, one of the biggest

trends among all of our expert authors is that each and every one of them has perfect hindsight. Every one of them would do things differently and have made more mistakes than they'd like to admit.

Just as Susanne discusses, so many webpreneurs get so caught up in building the site, writing the book or creating the product that they have spent all their energy (time and/or money) on getting the project done that they forget this is just the beginning of the business - now you have to market it.

It's a bit like planning a vacation: you spend all this time, effort, energy and money, planning, getting ready, getting some things paid for in advance (like hotel reservations or plane tickets) ... but if you've forgotten to leave yourself time to dream about how much fun the trip will be, or if you've not set aside spending money to go out and actually enjoy the destination you've just gone to.... then...? What was the point?

Or, to think of it another way, building a business is a bit like getting married or having a baby. The corporate marketers of the world are so busy "selling us" all the things we "need" to have for the Big Day (or bringing the baby home the first time) that we as a society often forget that there's a whole lifetime commitment here that's often over looked. If we spent as much time discussing the "marriage" (as an example) as we do discussing the WEDDING, how much would married life be different today?

The same holds true for building a business: we often talk about the "getting there" activities - research, building a site, etc. that we often forget that equal portions of effort need to be focused on "staying there" kinds of activities (managing your web-business, disaster recovery or data backup management, product life cycle management, customer relations management, etc), leaving some room and energy for the future - and daring to dream big a bit.

But for some of you who are reading this, building this business might be entirely on a shoestring budget. The idea of getting to the "end" of the development of your business and then yet to still need to come up with more funds to market the business is enough to send anyone running for the nearest Employment Agency. That's the beauty of learning from real experts with real advice: Susanne's addressed that for you right here.

For more information about this author, or to learn more about how to start your own web-based business, go to www.mcmoodycrawford.com. There you can also sign up for our newsletter and announcements about our upcoming events.

ABOUT RACHEL ROFE

If you knew Rachel Rofe just 10 years ago, you would've never thought this extremely shy, extremely overweight woman would have been able to turn things around in her life the way she has. In the span of five years, since Rachel has been in online full time, she has helped thousands of students, authored a book, sold two businesses, and has been featured in Woman's World, Entrepreneur, and Fox News.

The best part is, Rachel does all of this while traveling the world. To date, she's been to 49 of the 50 states, lived all over the US, and exotic locales such as Rio de Janeiro and Buenos Aries.

She credits her Internet marketing profession for her mobile dream lifestyle.

8

A TIME TRAVELER'S LETTER TO SELF: CAUTION, LIFE CHANGES AHEAD

by RACHEL ROFE
www.RachelRofe.com

Date: Five Years Ago

Dear Rachel:

I am coming to you, five years later, with information that will completely change the course of your life.

If you follow this, you'll be even happier, more fulfilled, richer, and make more of an impact in five years' time than if you hadn't heeded my advice.

That is a <u>promise</u>.

Sure, you'll have a good life without listening to me. But I know what you're capable of so don't settle for "good", or even "great". You could have a LEGACY behind you in five years from now.

Now, I know you don't listen all the time. J . So while I could tell you thousands of things you could to change your life, I've picked only the most important three. These are CRUCIAL!

Do these three things and your life will be exponentially happier:
* Focus
* Outsource
* Build a list

I'm going to tell you why each of these is so important and why you absolutely MUST listen to me on them.

Focus

First of all, focus is HUGE. I know how easy it is to get excited by all the latest and greatest shiny ideas. But they're not serving you. All they do is take you off-course, get you frustrated, and make you less money.

Here's a quote to live your life by: "If you chase two rabbits, both will escape."

You know this inherently. You know that when you focus on one goal, you can achieve it very easily. But when you're splitting your attention amongst a lot of things, NOTHING ends up getting finished well.

It's like multi-tasking. Do you know how many studies there are telling you how horrific multi-tasking is? It's FAR better to do ONE thing, get it done, and then move on to the next.

You'll feel better about being more productive. You won't have that never-ending feeling of anxiety, thinking there's more to get done, because you'll be USED to doing one thing at a time. You'll have so much more internal peace.

You'll make a lot more money too.

There's going to be a time when you're doing pretty well financially. And if you keep going the route you're going, you're going to end up LOSING it.

Trust me on this: you'll get on a bunch of mailing lists. You'll be bombarded by "opportunities". You're going to get all these bright, shiny ideas... and you're going to abandon what's making you money and watch your income plummet down.

I know what you're thinking – "Why would I do that? That sounds stupid! Why would I squash a good thing?"

Well, Rachel... common sense ain't so common.

You're going to get greedy. You're going to think, "Sure, I'm making good money now... but I could make even MORE, with less work!"

Don't do it.

Focus on one thing until you have it running on autopilot. (We'll talk about outsourcing soon.) Do NOT abandon a project midway just because other people tell you there are better/easier ways to make money.

(And that's another thing... *don't be so gullible!*)

I beg of you: pick something and stick with it. Get is systemized and make it into an autopilot stream. CUT OFF DISTRACTIONS.

Do you know that if you would spend one or two hours of FOCUSED time towards your goals, you would get as much done as you normally do in a 10-12 hour day?

Get off MySpace, LiveJournal, or whatever else is distracting you right now. Put 100% of your energy into your goals. Keep your eye on the prize.

If you're having trouble figuring out how to complete your goals, here's a neat method I learned from Gina Gaudio-Graves:

Buy a 3-subject notebook where you list out your yearly goals. For example, maybe your first goal is to make $10k/month from a project.

Break down how you can achieve those goals in three to six month increments (like having 500 people pay $20/month.)

In the first section, list daily to-do items where you break your second section down even more.

In short: figure out whatever you want, break it down into bite-size increments, and IMPLEMENT it.

I can't beg you enough to PLEASE stop jumping on every bandwagon. Only buy products that are relevant to your goals. See things through.

After you get each stream on autopilot you'll be able to move to the next thing. And if you fail on a project, no problem. You'll have money from your other efforts to fall back on.

You might be thinking, "How do I know when I'm focusing too much? What happens if something is destined for failure?"

There's going to be a point when you have to follow your intuition. There's definitely a fine line between giving up and knowing that most of your best manifestations come through in the 11th hour.

The universe IS going to challenge you and ask you to prove that you really want things.

But again: if you build up some income streams that are systemized, you'll have time to fail on other projects. It won't matter as much.

Coming from that place puts you in a place of POWER.

When you're running from opportunity to opportunity, money will not be as prevalent. You'll be working from "paycheck to paycheck" and you'll be focused on survival. You'll be desperate and in fear mode. You'll wreak havoc on your body, being completely stressed. You'll gain weight, you'll feel anxious, and you'll be miserable.

And you'll NEVER be able to make the impact you want to, and help other people. How could you help other people when you can't even take care of yourself?

If any of those income streams fall through (and the one you have right now will)... you want to have a back-up plan.

Work smarter, not harder... FOCUS on an income stream at a time, don't distract yourself, and then move to the next thing.

This is the #1 most important thing you could do.

And you know, the smartest people you will ever meet are people who are SIMPLE. They don't over-think things. They work on one thing, over and over, until it's done.

Please... don't try to outsmart your common sense.

Now, at this point you might be a little annoyed with me. We both know you're much more of an idea person. Focusing long-term isn't that easy for you, and doing the same thing every day drains your soul.

Stay with me because nobody said YOU need to do everything.

Outsource

I just asked you to get your ideas set up into income streams. You can certainly outsource anything you don't want to do.

And here's the great thing: ALMOST EVERYTHING CAN BE SYSTEMIZED IF YOU'RE WILLING TO THINK OUT OF THE BOX.

Remember, you've come to this world to do a lot more than just work. You're here to make an impact, to change lives, and to leave the world better than you left it.

Do you think Oprah has time to cook her food, clean her house, and do her laundry? Do you think the President has time to answer every email that comes his way?

Absolutely not.

And if they wasted time doing this, they wouldn't be able to make the impact they have.

They outsource. And you should too.

Don't be a tactician. Don't build up an ego, thinking nobody can do things as well as you can. Even if they can't… who cares? Your happiness and well being is FAR more important than a few dollars. Let other people do what you hate and you can focus on the fun things.

(By the way, you will NEVER enjoy sitting on the computer all day.)

You can get a lot more done when you divvy up your work.

Three people working on one project will get it done a LOT faster than 1 person. (And in my experience, three people will get things done more than 3x faster.)

I know you're concerned about paying money for things. You feel gluttonous. You don't know why you should pay for something when you could do it yourself. And if, by God's grace, you DO outsource something… you try to find the cheapest people available: STOP IT!

Stop spending so much time thinking about how you can SAVE money, and instead focus on how you can EARN money.

It'll save you a lot of time, put you in a much lighter place, and make you much more money.

Nine times out of 10, if you go with the cheapest outsourcer, you're going to regret it. You'll have to explain instructions over and over, you'll have to fix things yourself, or you'll get second-rate work you can't use.

You can create whatever money you need to outsource. Honestly… if you needed $25,000 in a week for some kind of crucial medical transplant, you'd create it. Surely you can raise a few hundred extra bucks.

Spend money on people who can help you tremendously. Figure out what your goals are and hire the people who can help you achieve them.

If for some reason you absolutely cannot outsource, there are a few things you can do:
1. Do things yourself and set aside a portion of the income you earn into outsourcers.
2. See if there's a quality person who is open to receiving a portion of your revenues instead of paying them a full salary right now.
3. Get a partner who complements you and is willing to do what you don't want to.

Partners are actually a PHENOMENAL idea, Rachel. I know you think you can do everything, but let's get clear on the fact that you're not perfect.

You do have a few challenges.

You don't like long-term thinking, you're inconsistent, and doing the same thing over and over drives you crazy.

I know it sounds crazy, but there are people who are NOT like that. And working with them will help balance you out and make you MUCH happier.

I'm not saying to outsource everything to a partner, or that you need partners for everything… I'm telling you to get clear on what you do and don't enjoy and to leverage other people as best you can.

Whether you're working with an outsourcer or a partner, please take my advice and START SLOW.

Work with them on a project first, then maybe another, then another. Don't get excited and hire – or partner with - people right away.

I know you always want to see the best in people but sometimes they're not what they seem.

Please take some time before you promise people full time jobs or long-term partnerships.

Giving away a portion of your income to a partner, or money to an outsourcer, might seem like a "loss". But that's scarcity based short-term thinking.

By getting rid of the things you don't like doing, you'll be much happier.

More customers will be attracted to you (and in today's day and age most people buy because of WHO you are, way more than WHAT you say).

Speaking of people buying from you, this brings me to my last point.

Build a buyers' list.
Most marketers I know say that if they lost everything and could only get one asset back, they would want their list.
A list is pretty important. Here's why:
- It's MUCH easier to market to existing customers who know, like, and trust you than it is to acquire new ones.
- A customer list is basically a license to create cash on demand. When you have a list of people who trust you, and you sell them something, they will BUY from you.
- There are all kinds of variables outside of your control. You might lose your advertising source, your website might shut down, or you might lose your PayPal account. If you have a list, you'll still be able to make money. You get to gain control through it.
- You're going to create a few businesses in your next couple of years. You'll get tired of them. Having a list increases the selling value of your business by a LOT.

There are many ways in which you can build a list. We'll go over a couple of them. Do as many of them as you like. The more you do, the more money you'll make.

Create multiple revenue streams

And please create a list for as many of your income streams as possible. (Or have your outsourcer do it.)

Option #1: Joint Ventures

Remember when I told you not to try and do everything yourself?

Joint ventures are a prime example of leveraging other people.

Here's how a joint venture works: find a business owner with customers who would want to buy your products. Offer their customers a special deal, and give the business owner a commission for all the customers they refer over.

It's a win/win situation – you get more buyers added to your list and the business owner gets money.

Don't worry about giving up 50% or even more commissions. Think long-term. That list is GOLD.

Option #2: Reward people for referring your products

There may be people who don't have customer lists yet, but they do have a few friends who they'd like to refer to your product.

Reward them for doing so.

Have some kind of reward system, or affiliate program, where you pay people in order to have them refer customers to you.

It only makes sense. When potential customers come to you via people they trust, they'll be much more likely to buy from you.

Offer a great commission and treat the people who refer customers to you very well.

Option #3: Create content

Content is also very big. If you – or your outsourcer – can come up with one piece of content every day to increase your reach, you will be EXTREMELY happy down the line.

The more valuable information you have out there means there are more people who will come across your path. Consequently there will be more people who know you, like you, and want to buy products from you.

The temptation is going to be to put out a product, make money, build a list, and then assume you don't need to do any more work.

That's not true.

Some customers are going to drop off. They might not be interested any more, might change their email addresses, or life might get in the way.

By creating content you'll ensure a steady flow of new customers to your business.

As you know, there is a TON of information out in the world. There are different opinions on how many exposures people need before they purchase from you, but it's at LEAST four or five.

That means you need as many "entry points" for people to learn about you as possible.

Creating content could mean posting on social media, writing blog posts, writing articles, or creating products.

Give away your best knowledge for free. Expect that people will appreciate that and reciprocate by buying your products.

I promise... it works.

Did you know that some of the biggest companies in the world actually LOST money in the beginning? They gave away free gift certificates and products in hopes that they would get their name out there.

It worked.

(You'll see how huge they are five years from now.)

The other thing you can do is just tell stories about what's going on in your life. The more people know about you, the closer they'll feel to you. The closer they feel to you, the more they'll want to be around – and buy from you.

This world is getting VERY noisy.

People have countless options for everything.

And less than 5% of people actually buy based off of logic. The overwhelming of them majority buy off of EMOTION.

So when they get to know about you, and they like you, they'll be way more likely to buy from you.

You fall "victim" to this too, you know.

There'll be one day you'll be looking for a personal trainer in San Diego. You're going to see hundreds of trainers you can work with. The one you'll end up hiring is the one who had a blog.

You'll see some of her fitness tips, learn about her story, and see how she got into such great shape very quickly after having a baby.

You'll also find people down the line who keep popping up on social media. You'll buy their products to see what the fuss is about.

I promise you, taking 30 minutes to write a blog post instead of hanging out on a social networking site will reward you tenfold down the line.

In conclusion...
So Rachel... I know this whole conversation might freak you out a little bit. You probably never expected the future you to come back and talk to you. But please, trust me. I know what's in your highest good.

The 3 things I mentioned could change your entire life.

By focusing on one income stream at a time, you'll be able to actually finish things and have something tangible to show for your efforts.

You're going to get an obsession for travel and you're going to need some way to fund it.

By outsourcing, you'll get to live a life you actually enjoy. You won't have to be worried about constantly doing everything and you'll be able to get a LOT more done.

And when you build a buyers' list, you'll be building security. This entrepreneurial world can be pretty risky sometimes.

It only makes sense to do everything you can to put the odds in your favor. I love you, very much, and hope you take me up on my advice. I guarantee it'll ensure you a successful and happy life.

With love,
Rachel

Editors' note

Rachel's "letter" to her younger self shows each of us how we might coach ourselves to do different things based on the information we have now. Her directive to develop your focus boils down to one of the core concepts threaded throughout this book: Focus. Focus on what you want. Do your research. Do you know what you want? Who are you and what are your skills: how do they fit into your brand of who you are and what you want your company to be?

Stepping forward from that base of knowledge then helps you to triage the deluge of information that comes at every Internet marketer. Ask yourself each time there is a product, a webinar, conference or even that you are told about
- *What is this going to give me that will help me accomplish my business goals?*
- *Will it help me make more money? Save money? Or help me run my business faster, better, smarter?*
- *Does it contribute or bring value to my brand?*

If it doesn't help you in one of these areas... then why are you doing it?

If you're not sure - take some time before you buy.

Remember, just as Rachel demonstrates for "Younger Rachel" - these are all marketing messages. It's the objective of these other marketers to get you to buy their product.

Your objective is to screen each and every opportunity against how it will help you meet your business goals. If you've done your homework - the research, the business planning, etc., that we've touched on through out this book - you'll be able to decipher which items don't fit, which items do fit but you have a better "route" on your road map for getting to where you are, and which items might provide a better solution and get you to your destination even faster.

Don't be afraid to take in information - but hold it at arm's length before you embrace it (buy). Listen to what the marketing messages are. There are legitimate, extraordinary business people -- just like Rachel and our other expert authors - who really can be a lighthouse for your business, warning you against rocky shoals and giving you the advice you need to succeed. There are also hucksters who don't care if you crash against the rocks after they've gotten your money.

Captain your business; Learn from Rachel and the others who know how to bring a project successfully home.

For more information about this author, or to learn more about how to start your own web-based business, go to www.mcmoodycrawford.com. There you can also sign up for our newsletter and announcements about our upcoming events.

ABOUT MARLON SANDERS

Marlon Sanders innovated a number of techniques that are now commonplace online, including the 12-step formula for writing sales letters, 2-page web site model, structure of modern download pages, and the list goes on and on. He was a major contributor to what is just accepted practice in today's Internet marketing.

The seminars he spoke at in Boulder, Colorado with Jonathan Mizel and Declan Dunn hold a special place in Internet marketing lore and were attended by many who went on to become Internet marketing "gurus."

In addition, he has spoken at over 120 seminars around the world including Australia, Bermuda, Kauai, London and Birmingham in the UK, and all over the U.S. -- including Seattle, San Francisco, Las Angeles, St. Louis, Chicago, Nashville, Philadelphia, San Diego, Houston, Dallas, Sacramento, New York, and Cincinnati.

He was a featured at the Next Internet Millionaire seminar produced by Joel Com and has had the honor and pleasure of speaking at Big Seminar not once but twice and most recently spoke at Frank Garon's event in London.

Marlon invented several product categories that have become popular such as Push Button Letter Generators and Dashboards of various types. He's perhaps most known for "The Amazing Formula That Sells Products Like Crazy" which was one of the first digitally delivered e-books on Internet marketing to capture the attention of the marketplace.

Marlon's affiliate program for his products has appeared numerous times in the top 10 list at associateprograms.com

9

TAKING CARE OF BUSINESS: IT'S YOUR JOB #1

by MARLON SANDERS
www.MarlonSanders.com

I want to share with three things I wish I'd known over the years that would have made my life easier, increased my wealth and expanded my business faster.

I've had the good fortune of selling millions of dollars of e-books, courses and training online. At the same time, I could have made even more if I knew these things.

1. The absolute importance of watching and tracking the results of major changes like a hawk

Anytime you make a major change in your business, marketing, staff or operations, you absolutely must monitor the results of that change.

According to the book *Breakthrough Business Results with MVT* by Charles Holland, QualPro and its clients tested over 150,000 ideas in 13,000 projects during 22 years. Only one in four ideas improved results, while 53% of the ideas made no difference and 22% actually hurt the results.

That means half the changes you make don't help you get the results you want. And one in five times, what you think helps your business actually hurts it!

That's why you need to track and monitor the results of changes. I speak from painful personal experience.

For example, when the U.S. Congress passed the Can-Spam legislation, I had to combine my email lists hosted at two separate companies to one company. The law said people had to be able to unsubscribe from all your lists at once.

In online marketing, we use a service called auto responders that allow us to broadcast messages to our email subscribers. I used two separate services. But after Can-Spam, I had to reduce that to one.

The problem is, I forgot to monitor sales after making that change. If I had done that, I would've seen that our sales dropped 30% overall and probably would have decided to switch to the other service.

Later on, when I was pouring over graphs of our sales, my eyes about jumped out of my head when I saw the massive drop in sales. Ouch! That hurt.

The problem we have is the speed of business. Product life cycles are a fraction of what they used to be, even for the largest, most savvy companies. It's easy to get caught up in the pressures of the day-to-day grind and forget to do really important things like track the results of major changes you make in your business.

Here's another example: We market our training programs using an affiliate program, where our partners link to our products from their websites and blogs and make a commission when a sale happens.

In the early days, the software we used for our affiliate program had only the most basic features. It worked great. But boy, you didn't have a lot of bells and whistles on it.

That's when we ran across our dream software. Holy smokes! It had all kinds of tricked out reports, bells and whistles galore. The additional benefits persuaded us to move 25,000 affiliates from the existing software to the new one.

Now, if you know much about people, you know they're a little strange. On the one hand, they love new stuff. On the other, they hate change. Because change takes time. And time is something they don't have enough of.

Which is to say that our affiliates weren't crazy about this move. Not only that, we found out after the move that the software didn't work as we thought. What a nightmare. Finally, after custom programming, we got everything working reasonably well.

Except that in all the hustle and bustle of the move, and trying to communicate with 25,000 affiliates, believe it or not, we forgot to watch our monthly sales like a hawk.

Later on, after pouring over stats again, I saw that our affiliate sales took a nosedive when we moved to the software and never came back. That was about a $200,000 a year mistake. The problem is, by the time I became aware of the sales dive, it was almost too late to switch back.

Ultimately, this year we moved to a new software program and I don't regret it one bit. I also researched the move much more carefully and watched the results after the move.

In the tech-driven business like online marketing training, the software is never perfect. You never have the ultimate solution. You learn to live with compromises between speed, ease of use, and power.

Software changes can make or break you. Our new software platform has its share of issues. People love or hate it. I made our decision based on my observation of sales increases from my friends who moved to the platform before I did.

Two different friends increased sales by $50,000 a month very quickly. That's a pretty big increase for small online businesses.

If you're following me so far, the question becomes "What changes do you track, how do you track them and what are the pitfalls to avoid?"

Let's tackle those questions one-by-one.

What changes do you track?

A business grows by removing limitations to growth in four key areas: Product, marketing, personnel, and operations.

That means in order to grow, you won't be stagnant. You'll be making changes as you try to remove limitations. And, as I pointed out early, one in five of those changes will hurt your sales instead of improve them!

The end result is, when you take action to remove limitations you're experiencing in your product creation or delivery, operations, personnel, or marketing, you better monitor those changes.

But how?

I'm sure you're familiar with Edward Deming. If you aren't, I'll put it this way: He's the dude that helped Japan turn into an economic powerhouse after the war.

Deming used concepts to like "run charts" and "analysis of variance" to identify which results were significant and which ones weren't. The point he made was that without a scientific way to study charts, you can run around in circles fixing things that aren't broken.

And you know what? He was right? You know what else? I don't use run charts or statistical analysis methodology like ANOVAs, but I should. In the ideal world, I'd use them. And if you know how to use them, you absolutely should.

I have all the math acumen of a pet rock. So what do I do? I look for elephant tracks. You know, numbers or variations that are large enough, you don't need a run chart to know, "Wow, that's significant!"

In other words, I dominantly to try get the big things right. I don't employee statisticians and people who know how to do run charts. Maybe someday I will. Today I don't. I'm guessing you probably don't either and that the speed of your business is something like mine.

Blink and things have changed.

So here's what I do. I monitor sales and other key indicators monthly. When the elephant tracks appear, I fly into action. According to life expectancy tables, I only have 240 months left on this planet.

That's my big picture. I focus on it.

What are the pitfalls?

One of the big pitfalls is only looking for changes that make sales go down. What about the accidental changes that make them go up?

Fortunately, sometimes sales go up by dumb luck. When you find the reason for that dumb luck and do it deliberately, it becomes smart luck.

The other pitfall is forgetting to look at the numbers.

Which brings me quite logically to the second thing I wish I'd known...

2. How to divide my day by core success factors and focus on them daily.

I'm about to shake up your life... in a positive way. I'm about to give your creativity and productivity a giant injection.

I debated whether or not I should include this. Time management or anything to do with it is a highly personal topic. Everyone seems to have a system that works for him or her. I ran across a gem of a method I wish I'd known about and used over the years.

I'm using it right this very minute as I write this. Other than the one source I'm going to reference, I've never seen anyone else teach this. That's why I decided to go ahead and share it here.

The idea I'm going to present to you is not my own. I learned it from a little booklet called *Neo-Tech Control* by Mark Hamilton (ASIN # B00072DLYI). Just so you know, Neo-Tech has more than its share of critics. I personally liked more than one of their books. Some people, according to Google results, obviously didn't. That's a whole lesson in marketing right there: One man's trash is another man's treasure.

With that said, if you want a really terrific idea I wish I'd done all my business life, here it is:

1. Figure out the major things you need to do every day to have a successful business
2. Block out time every day for those activities
3. For example, here is how I have today blocked out:
    -   WRITING – 9 p.m. – 12 p.m.
    -   CALLS -- 12:30 - 12:45
        o   Contact Quick Sales System
        o   Find and call Infusionsoft Consultant
    -   OPERATIONS – 1 – 1:45
        o   Quick Sales System
        o   Edward Upsell
        o   How did Lee do delivery email?
            o   Find Infusionsoft consultant to look at order problems
            o   Buy gift certificates

- o   Buy iPads
- • ACCOUNTING – 2 - 2:45
  - o   Find exported PayPal expenses
  - o   Plan WEEKLY accounting report by categories
  - o   Expenses Calendar
- • MARKETING NUMBERS -- 3 – 3:30
  - o   Facebook ad costs vs. returns
  - o   Marketing Numbers Report
- • PROMO – 3:30
  - o   Plan AF Promotion
- • RESEARCH -- Evening
  - o   Read Society of Secrets
  - o   Research software for global biz
  - o   jack stack

Obviously, those tasks don't mean much to you. But they do to me.

The overall concept is that you assign a time slot each day to an area of responsibility like marketing or accounting. You work on that area for the same amount of time each day.

At the end of the assigned time, you move onto the next area of responsibility. Period. The only exceptions are emergencies or mission critical tasks.

What most people do is write out tasks for the day on a schedule. But the schedule never goes as planned. If one task takes too long, the whole day is thrown off.

You never get in a routine because the tasks change every day. You never have the chance to get in a flow because your schedule always changes.

Contrast this with working on the same areas of your business every day.

Here's why I say this would have had a major impact on my results over the years.

Every single day you block out time to focus on the areas that are critical to the success of your business.

Just this simple change in routine and mindset brings up a slew of objections: "Marlon, aren't you supposed to delegate all those tasks and only do what you're best at?"

Yes. Absolutely. That's what I've done most of my career. I read "Emyth" by Michael Gerber a long time ago. Loved that book. And before you can document processes the way Gerber teaches, you need to first have the successful processes in place. Not only that, but from my experience, absentee owners don't a business make.

Unless and until you have every system documented, monitored and humming like a machine, you might want to try the method I'm suggesting here. To live the four-hour workweek, you've really got to have lock-tight systems and a favorable economy and market.

"Marlon, isn't this just Steven Covey revamped?"

We all love Steven Covey. Great ideas. But this actually is a very different method. Covey had you set business roles and plan tasks related to those roles each week, being sure to include activities that are important but not urgent.

The problem is, every day those activities change. And if tasks expand the time allotted, the important but not urgent activities get shoved to the backburner.

Don't get me wrong. Tons of people have benefited from the Franklin-Covey method. And as long as you get the activities done at the end of the week, that's all that matters.

With that said, I'm a creature of habit. Like it. Hate it. Despise it. You probably are too. By doing the same area of responsibility every day at the same time for the same amount of time, you develop a habit.

For me, accounting is one of those things I resist doing. But by having an accounting focus time every day, it becomes a habit.

I'll give you a practical example. In the highly stimulating, ever changing environment we live in, focusing is difficult. Non-stop waves of events clamoring for your attention come at you from every side. You check your Facebook, or someone instant messages you for this or that, the phone rings, an email shows up. By the end of the day, you did a lot but nothing got done.

By having assigned times daily that you stick to every day, if an operational issue comes up, instead of losing your focus and working on it that very moment, you can confidently say, I'll call you at this time.

It happened to me today. An employee brought up an issue about our upsell process (the system by which we offer an additional value to a person who just made a purchase from us) that needed my input. Normally, I would have dropped what I was doing and got drug down into the issue, totally destroying my focus.

Instead, I knew my operations time was at 1. So I said, "I'll call you about that at 1." And I did it like clockwork.

Another one that comes up is checking social sites. To say that spending any time on a social site, such as Facebook or any other, is a waste doesn't make sense. This chapter is a result of making contact with a friend on a social site.

However, what normally happens is the thought pops into your head, "Oh my goodness, I haven't checked XYZ site today." You drop what you're doing, interrupt your flow, and get sidetracked.

I have that same problem with checking online news. I'm somewhat of an online news addict.

Today, when the thought leaped into my attention zone, "You need to check Facebook," I opened the information manager I use, Time and Chaos, and I put my note in there to check Facebook during my marketing time.

I haven't figured out how to handle online news yet. But I know I'm going to assign it to one of my time slots or only do it after my time windows are finished.

Today, during my operations time, I worked on our upsell process. Normally, I'd be rushed because of all the other tasks I'm in a hurry to get done.

But today, I relaxed and worked effortlessly with my employee on the issue. Why? Because I knew I had allotted the issue to my operations time.

Working on new products is something I tend to do in a massive crash course for a week, two weeks or a month. My last product was one of our famous Dashboards. And it about did me in working on it.

Seriously!

I underestimated the volume of work it'd take to finish it. The problem with doing a two week or month long crash course on anything is that all your other responsibilities tend to fall by the wayside.

You probably don't take the time to check up thoroughly on the current numbers of your ads or affiliate promotions. You may even skip those responsibilities because you're so preoccupied with your crash course project, whatever it may be.

Then, when you finally finish your crash course item, other areas have now crashed and are in serious need of tender loving care, or even rehab. You cram a whole lot activities into your day planner the night before, wake up, suck down some coffee, stare at this endless list, and feel the sudden urge to do anything other than tackle that laundry list of tasks.

In a huge burst of insight, you realize that time management book told you to prioritize things as A's, B's or C's. You zip through that gnarly list, prioritize everything and jump to work on you're A list. What are the chances that you made A's out of the things you don't like to do? You probably prioritized all the things you like to do.

Or, let's say you first go through the list and cherry pick all the important but not urgent tasks and put those on your calendar. For me, I can tell you that there's a snowball's chance in July that I put a balanced representation on that list of the tasks that drive my business.

In other words, I doubt that the important but not urgent tasks would include a mix of marketing, personnel, operations, and product development tasks.

For me, chances are 80% of those suckers end up being marketing oriented since that's what I see the most value in. At heart, I'm a marketer.

Let's recast that scenario using the new approach.

Every day, you work on your product for X amount of time. As soon as that one is done, the very next day, you're onto the next one. If you stick with this religiously, you totally eliminate "project binging" and enjoy a saner, better-paced business. Your creativity soars because you aren't under intense deadline pressure. The quality of your work skyrockets.

Every day, you assign a set amount of time to the other categories of tasks that drive your business.

Of course, there is a catch.

Sticking to daily time slots isn't easy. They key is to do it because you see the benefits to you and your business of doing it. Not because you're supposed to do it that way.

If you're really crystal clear on the benefits of it, you absolutely can do it.

I transitioned to mistake number two from mistake number one by pointing out that one of the pitfalls of number one is simply forgetting to check your numbers.

If you follow the method I just outlined, you'll have a set segment of time daily where you work on accounting. You can include reviewing stats in your accounting section.

I addition, I started out mistake number two with this statement:

I don't know anyone else who teaches this exact method. The closest I've heard of is a concept called "Timeboxing."

But if you look it up on Wikipedia, it isn't the same thing. Almost every time management method I've seen is task-based. You start with your list of tasks.

This is completely different. You start with your areas of responsibilities and block off the same time slot and the same amount of time daily to work on that area. That's very different from simply grouping tasks because the next day, you may have completely different groups of tasks.

Mark Hamilton teaches a lot of nuance, twists and advanced concepts. I'm not here to steal his thunder. I'm a marketer, not a time management expert.

I can tell you this method will absolutely increase my profits substantially over the next year. And the only cost was a journal to write down my stuff in.

Now let's move on to the third thing I wish I'd known...

3. The vastly accelerating speed of business
I teach Internet marketing. I've done quite well over the years doing that and have had the good fortune to speak around the world at over 120 seminars.

In other words, I'm not new at the game, nor am I inexperienced. Yet, I managed to vastly underestimate the accelerating speed of business.

In other words, the crystal clear advantage you have today may be gone tomorrow. The celebrity attention you receive today can be gone tomorrow.

The product that sells gangbusters today can dwindle tomorrow.

Here are a few things you might have noticed:
1. Product lifecycles are a fraction of what they used to be, even for the largest of companies. In the early days of Internet marketing (1997-2003), you could produce a product and have it sell month after month without a lot of effort. In 2011, you can get sales after your launch but you have to plan and work for them.
2. Competitors are faster, smarter and better funded. They're willing to invest more time, money and energy to get sales.
3. You have a shorter window of time to bring a new product to market before your competitors do.
4. Online sales videos, processes, websites and blogs all improve in quality and design at a rapid rate.

Should we go grab a gun, stick it to our head, and get it over with?

Heck no!

But you do need to dig in and be the best that you can be.

If you've read Michael Porter's *Competitive Advantage* (my hands-down favorite of his books), then you know that his theme is how to create a sustainable competitive advantage in business.

But he wrote that magnificent work back in 1985. We didn't have iPhones or iPads back then. I think the fundamental truths he outlined still carry weight. At the same time, there's a point at which the only sustainable competitive advantage is the ability to create competitive advantages faster than the competition. How crazy is that?

This isn't something most newbies coming into online marketing understand. It isn't something you relate to unless you run a business. In which case you may be shaking your head right now.

His contention in the book was that there are only two basic types of competitive advantage – cost leadership and differentiation. In differentiation, you choose one attribute and serve it up better than anyone else.

Hopefully, there's some aspect that makes your point of difference difficult to copy by competitors. That's called a "barrier to entry."

All this is a bunch of lingo if you're new to marketing or business. I'll try to boil it down to simple terms.

If you come out with an idea or feature that sells like hotcakes, your competitors are going to knock you off and offer the same thing before you can blink an eye unless there's something that keeps them from doing it.

That something is what marketers call a "barrier to entry."

For example, I created a concept called "Evergreen Internet Marketing." I differentiated on the attribute of Evergreen.

Other marketers picked up on that and now call their products Evergreen also. Unfortunately, there's no barrier to entry. Anyone can call his or her product Evergreen. Not that I'm complaining. I sucked a lot of sales out of the word Evergreen before others caught on and knocked off the attribute.

I created another concept called Dashboards. They're a set of 6 icons across and 6 rows down. You click on an icon and are served up a set of 1, 2, 3, 5 numbers with instructions. These Dashboards have held their differentiation from 2001 until this year when a competitor knocked off the concept.

Of course, I anticipated that happening long ago. I considered destroying their product launch with my own maneuvers but better judgment restrained me from that. I do have a plan I'll put into place.

I was the first major Internet marketing teacher to use super high quality pro photos in my web sites. But it didn't take more than a few months for a few others to copy that.

If you've ran any kind of a business before, you know exactly what I'm talking about. And it probably drives you a little batty like it does me. Or like it does Apple. They have what? A two-month lead-time on a new product before the knock-offs from other companies hit the shelves?

So what can be done about this?

How have I responded? How can you respond?

I want to introduce you to a concept called "merchandising offers." I didn't invent this idea. Like most of my other ideas, I borrowed them from others and adapted them to fit my business.

This particular idea came from T.J. Rohleder. I'd call T.J. the King of

Business Opportunities.

Basically, I'm a merchant of ideas. I'll take ideas from the Harvard Business Journal, cults, religions, and other industries – anyplace I can find them. I think I learned that from Jay Abraham a long time ago. He said to take ideas from other industries. So I did.

Anyway, like Neo-Tech, T.J. has his fans and his critics, some of whom are prominent when you do a Google search.

The reason I bring up T.J. is he explains merchandising offers better than anyone, anywhere. I've read at least 5,000 books if not more. It's not unusual for me to spend $25,000 or more buying books and courses to feed my brain in a year.

And I can tell you with confidence, no one does a better job of explaining this than T.J. But I'll do my own version of it here.

The solution to the incredible speed of business is to do a much better job than your competition at creating highly attractive offers and merchandising them. T.J. says we don't sell products or services.

We sell offers.

I think that's not only spot on, it's profound.

Look at it like dating. I'll explain this from a guy's perspective, since that's the only one I understand.

The product is you and your physical appearance. The offer is everything other than your physical appearance. How you talk. The confidence with which you carry yourself. The way you walk.

But beyond that, it's the invitation to take that girl of your dreams out on a boat to a beautiful lake and hang out with some other friends while you get a suntan. The sun. The water. Friends. Good times.

The girl sees you're a man of substance – you either own a boat or are clever enough to get one for a weekend. She sees that you're social – you have friends. She notices that you have a very healthy looking suntan and that you like physical activity, a sign of virility.

She sees you very differently than the guy on the street that whistles at her.

That's the difference between the product and the offer.

We're in the business of creating and merchandising or promoting and marketing offers that are more exciting than our competitors offer.

You can't always quickly change your product. But you can create an endless supply of new offers. For example, I have a product I'm revamping right now. My big change in the sales message will be to offer seven highly attractive new bonuses I've never offered before.

The offer includes the price, payment terms, bonuses, and guarantee -- the whole package. Your offer needs to be presented or merchandised better than your competitors' offers.

Think of the Mac commercials. They have a great product. And do a great job of selling the offer. If I were Microsoft, I would have played my cards a little differently. I'd run a commercial that looks like a Mac commercial. You have the nerdy PC guy and the super cool Mac dude. All of a sudden you hear CUT!

The commercial is over. The actors leave the studio. The PC guy wheels around in a Mercedes. The Mac dude can't start his junker. He says, "Dude, can I borrow a ride? My car is a junker because I spent all my money on my Mac computer!"

It's all about the presentation of the offer.

Let's say you own a little PC repair shop. You put a big yellow banner outside with black letters: PC Slow? Free Virus Scan.

That's your offer. Others will copy it. When that happens, you create a new banner:

Watch Your Computer On TV. Demo Inside.

It's all about the offer.

Cool, eh?

You may say, "That's great Marlon. But how does it apply to me?"

I have one more book for you. Jon Spoelstra wrote *Marketing Outrageously* and *Ice to Eskimos*. He was general manager for the Portland Trail Blazers NBA basketball team for 11 years and president of the New Jersey Nets.

When he became president of the New Jersey Nets, their local sponsorship revenue was $400,000. In three years he boosted that to $7 million. He increased ticket sales from $5 million to $17 million. And the market value of the team went from $40 million to $120 million.

How? He put together irresistible offers such as his White Castle family night where he sold a family ticket package – four tickets, four meals at White Castle hamburgers, a Nets cap, and a Nets basketball for $39.95!

The normal thinker would say the product is a basketball game. Jon turned the product into an offer of a family night package.

He sold a 7-game package where you got to see the top NBA players at the arena. The Nets had a bad record. But people would still show up to see megastars. If you need ideas on how to come up with creative offers, then you absolutely must read Jon's books.

Your brain will explode with new, highly profitable marketing ideas, offers and promotions.

I love marketing ideas. I'm a merchant of ideas. That's what I do. I find awesome marketing ideas wherever I can find them and deploy them in my business as highly stimulating offers to my customers.

That's my antidote to the speed of business. No longer will I underestimate it. Instead, I'll embrace it.

I'm a marketer. This is my destiny. That's what I do.

I hope that sharing with you a few painful mistakes I've made and the solutions I've developed shines a light along your path and makes it a bit brighter, clearer and easier to tread.

I bid you well.

Editors' note

Even "successful" marketers could have been "even MORE successful" if they had just tweaked a few things they'd done along the way.

As discussed by other expert authors, Marlon shows us the incredible importance of realizing the work is not over once you've written the book or launched the website.

The real work comes in managing your business - measuring each and every idea against your business ideal plan, seeing if ideas will get you to your desired goal faster, cheaper or smarter and then seeing if those ideas actually DID do what you thought they'd do.

Some "course changes" are almost impossible to recover from once you've made the decision. Even with the best of intentions and research, sometimes business decisions don't go as you'd planned them. The question is: what <u>can</u> you do at that point to get your ship back on course?

He echoes a vital reminder to us all about the importance of finding a way, a method or system - whatever works for you - to ensure you are doing the things that matter most to your business. Regardless of which system you follow - Franklin Covey, Aligned Thinking, Getting Things Done -- find what works, use it. Start creating your own cookbook or series of documented processes so that you do have the option of delegating given tasks to others. You'll quickly figure out which tasks can (and should) be outsourced, and which ones should or must be done by only you.

But he also speaks to important things that aren't as obviously "labeled" as things he'd do differently - but are vital to any webpreneur's success.

First, Marlon speaks to the idea of constantly learning, or "feeding your brain." You don't have to be earning a PhD or masters' to do this. But as a business person, you do need to be constantly learning, striving to understand more about business, learning more about your customers, analyzing what you're customers are doing, and finding ways to reinvest in yourself. The creative element you bring to any piece of information is the fundamental difference between you and the way any other "Joe-Marketer" or "Joe-Webpreneur" does it can be vastly different. So while Corporate American pays lip-service to touting how they "invest in their employees" or how "our employees are our most valuable asset" -- this is no longer an "option" in your new world as a web- or infopreneur.

Marlon's experiences also speak to the importance of constantly monitoring what trends are starting to happen in your world, and learning to anticipate those trends. How will a piece of legislation affect your business? What does the changing trend in Generation Xer's not having as many babies mean to me? While the economy might be "taking away" some kinds of business opportunities, is it creating others? Does the environmental movement mean anything to me, my business or my customers? Learning to be constantly on the

119

lookout for new trends and determining their impact to your business is a bit like forecasting the weather. There's a lot of science to it; there's some near misses. But when the big one hits.... because you've been watching the trends, preparing your business and its processes, you just might be able to take advantage of the winds of change.

For more information about this author, or to learn more about how to start your own web-based business, go to <u>www.mcmoodycrawford.com</u>. There you can also sign up for our newsletter and announcements about our upcoming events.

ABOUT DR. MANI

Dr. Mani Sivasubramanian is a heart surgeon and infopreneur who uses his Internet based information business to fund heart surgery for under-privileged children in India.

Dr. Mani teaches people just like you how to earn a steady online income based around what you love. He creates and sells e-books and information products that show you how to turn what you already know into cash in the bank. Since 1996, he has helped thousands of clients build a purpose-driven online business around their passions.

As an author of over 65 e-books and 2 print publications, Dr. Mani has influenced countless e-publishers, home business owners and Internet marketers with his powerful writing, insight and experience, and is an enthusiastic crusader of what's possible for small home business owners by effectively harnessing the power and reach of the World Wide Web.

His first print book, "Think, Write & Retire!" roared up the ranks to break into the "Hot 100" list within 24 hours of its launch. The book received critical acclaim from some of the biggest names in Internet marketing, and profits from the book launch funded 4 heart operations in full.

Among other things, Dr. Mani has been named as one of Seth Godin's '99 Purple Cows' for innovative and remarkable marketing, and FAST COMPANY magazine has profiled his philanthropy-fuelled approach to business. He has consistently ranked in the list of top 50 Internet marketing specialists at Gurudaq.com

He is also an energetic social entrepreneur, philanthropist and teacher. A firm believer in the concept of 'business with purpose', Dr. Mani ties in every element of his online work with a passion to help under-privileged children born with congenital heart defects.

His information business profits help to fund life-saving heart surgery for children with CHD. That was indeed the motivation behind launching his infoproduct enterprise more than 15 years ago. Heart surgery is expensive. Many of his patients come from poor families and cannot afford the cost of life-saving treatment. So Dr. Mani decided to try and help fund these costly operations through a combination of infoproduct sales and by seeking donations.

Since then, Dr. Mani's team of clients and donors has raised more than $150,000 that has funded heart surgery in 70 children, with many more to follow. His ambitious mission is to *make high quality heart health care accessible and affordable to every Indian child.*

You can learn more about Dr. Mani's non-profit work at www.CHDinfo.com and his infopreneur business at www.InfoProfitz.com or his blog at www.InternetInfopreneur.com/blog/

Some special reports written by Dr. Mani that you may enjoy are:

- *The Infopreneur Manifesto http://www.ThinkWriteRetire.com/TWRmanifesto.pdf*
- *The PASSION Manifesto (at ChangeThis) http://changethis.com/53.04.PassionManifesto*
- *Internet Infopreneur blog: http://feeds.feedburner.com/InformationMarketingMadeEasy*
- *Money.Power.Wisdom blog: http://feeds.feedburner.com/money-power-wisdom*

10

'BIG DOGS,' ARCHIMEDES, AND STRATEGIC THINKING

by MANI SIVASUBRAMANIAN, MD
http://www.ezinemarketingcenter.com/drmaniname/

Coming as I do from a family of professionals, with no entrepreneurial blood in it, and without access to anyone who ran a business or founded a start-up to contact for advice or opinion, my early attempts at building an information business on the Internet were interesting explorations in the dark!

Back in 1995, the Web was still in its infancy. There was little by way of information or guidance. Hardly anyone knew, with any kind of certainty, what the future of online business would be. With the medium itself serving as my only education (apart from the business books I devoured eagerly), much of the fumbling starts were just hopeful forays into what sounded like an exciting arena to explore.

The key to my success, then, lay more in the fact that I stuck to whatever I tried long enough for it to work!

Today, the problem is different. There is so much information, guidance and experience available everywhere that it is hard to know where to look, whom to follow and what to trust and believe in order to get a head start. And Internet business itself has grown diverse in an incredible way over two decades, spawning many different opportunities and encouraging innovation in so many dramatic ways, revolutionizing the way we think and do things - both online and off.

In this context, if I were starting out today, what are three things that I wish I'd known earlier to get an edge over my competition, and that would speed up my growth and success?

The first would be to understand the importance of branding.

Branding

Now in a traditional business sense, you'd imagine branding to be something only the "Big Dogs" do. Maybe you're telling yourself, "I'm not HP or Nike. Why do I need to bother about branding?"

Well, today, everyone is a brand. Not a mega-brand, perhaps. But surely a micro-brand. The brand called 'YOU'.

It's what makes you unique, differentiates you from the crowd of competitors, and sets you apart from anyone else who is in your niche or space. Your micro-brand is as meaningful and important as that of any other business that's a household name - with one difference.

Your reach may not be as extensive, but it's still as impactful - to your audience.

People you are reaching out to - as customers, as prospects, as leads, as students, as trainees - are all looking at you in light of your brand. What do you (and your business) stand for? What are you about? What is it that makes you special? What can they expect from you? How will they recognize and identify with you?

All these 'soft' components go into your brand.

Almost accidentally, I got this one element right when I started out. And that single asset has been responsible for helping sustain my online efforts for 15 years, leading to a scattered audience around the world becoming aware (in a positive light) about my name, and then my offerings in the information marketing space. It's responsible, in a sense, for my being invited to contribute to this book.

Look, a brand is a lot more than just a nice looking logo like Nike's swoosh, or a mission and vision statement that's a catchy jingle and sounds nice on radio or TV. A brand is a representation, to your marketplace, of the kind of person you are, or the kind of business you are, as presented over the medium of the Internet.

Your brand and the message it conveys must therefore be simple and clear, consistent and authentic, reflecting your core values and those of your business.

In the widely networked, socially connected online universe we are engaged in today, authenticity is your biggest asset, transparency is your biggest risk, and trust is your biggest benefit.

Rewarded with the trust of your audience, you can achieve just about any level of success you desire. It won't matter what your product or service is. It may not even matter that you slip up from time to time, or make a few bad decisions, or fail to deliver on a promise at times. Once your audience knows and trusts you, appreciates that you are always acting in their best interests, they will reward you richly with their business... for a long time to come.

Knowing what your brand stands for and living up to the expectations you set will automatically force you to play the "long game." No longer will you be tempted to self-destruct by the lure of "quick riches." You will shun the mindset of trying to scam unwary victims with unreal promises and hype. And you will have a frame of reference against which to match the big decisions in your business future.

In the virtual world of Internet business, where your digital persona is the most visible representation of your brand, having everything consistent and working together brings enormous synergy to your business efforts. Even without understanding the nuances of branding, you can incorporate it into your online business by being true to a set of values and being consistent in how you present them to your audience.

There are two articles that will help you better understand the critical role that branding plays in modern Web business. "The Brand Called YOU" by Tom Peters, first published in FAST COMPANY magazine in 1997, and "The Global Microbrand" by Hugh MacLeod, posted on the Gaping Void blog. I recommend these for anyone interested in branding and the Internet.

Leverage

It was the famous Greek philosopher and scientist Archimedes who said: "Give me a lever long enough and I will move the world!"

He was talking about the power of using levers, which shift energy from one point of a long rod to another, and by doing so, multiplying its effect many times over.

In our business (and indeed in our lives) we have access to incredible and amazing resources that we can leverage in powerful and effective ways. The problem is that we don't often recognize them and take advantage of that power.

In my own business, I stumbled onto the power of leverage only after listening to an eye-opening lecture by marketing guru Jay Abraham. With new insights, I looked into different components of my information business, which by then was five years old, and found some untapped assets that could explode my profitability.

Just that simple act of correctly identifying and tapping those assets literally doubled my bottom-line next year... and then re-doubled them again the next!

So, what are these assets and how to leverage them?

Often your most precious assets in an online business (just as with an offline business) are the intangibles. The relationships you have with your customers and subscribers. The networks you have built of suppliers, service providers, or marketing partners. The knowledge and expertise you have acquired from doing specific things in your business over years. The teams you have built or assembled to help with your projects.

All of these can be leveraged in a way that your new competitors cannot copy.

When my first website went live in 1996, it took almost six months before I consistently received 10 visitors a day. Today, when I launch a new website, I no longer have to wait for months, or even days. I can have a flood of visitors hitting my brand new site within hours (if not minutes) by leveraging my connections and assets.

The first e-book I wrote took me almost two years to sell 100 copies. Today, I can start writing one knowing that the first 100 copies will sell out in a week, if not sooner. That's because I can leverage contacts and past buyer lists quickly and effectively.

But what if you're just getting started?

This is exactly the nuance I wish I had known years back. You can employ leverage very profitably, even if you're just starting out with your online business!

The trouble is, every time we begin something new, in a different area, we approach it as if nothing else in our life from the past is relevant to it. And that's a big mistake. Often, things from your previous experiences can be brought to bear in any new venture and generate a big impact over a short time.

Let's say, for instance, that you've written a book and are looking to sell it online. Where a professional marketing course would teach you to try search engine optimization (SEO), run ads on ezines, get reviews, do guest blog posts and try article marketing, you'll probably get much better results by when you reach out to people who already know you and let them know you've written a book.

What's more, because these people already know YOU, they will happily tell their contacts, friends and colleagues, family and neighbors, who will then go out and buy your book. All this has become easier, faster and cheaper with the explosion of online social networks like Twitter, Facebook and Google+ giving anyone the opportunity to touch millions of people with a message that resonates.

Having an article published on a blog that reaches 100,000 readers will beat writing dozens of articles and getting them hosted on smaller websites with barely 100 readers in a month. And when that article is compelling and interesting to readers, they will tell even more people about it and word spreads virally, getting you even greater reach with no extra effort or expense.

Getting one popular newsletter publisher or forum owner to review your product or service can bring you more new customers than spending hundreds or thousands of dollars running paid ads. Partnering with someone who has a big list of past buyers can fast track the success of your newly launched product.

All these are examples of using leverage in your business.

What takes some effort and insight is to correctly identify the valuable assets that you either own or have access to. Think laterally. Go wide. See random connections. Get "out of the box." That way, you'll be able to make everything you do count, and have a bigger impact from every ounce of effort or cent of money you invest into growing your Internet business.

And putting leverage to work in every new initiative you set up can speed up your growth as well.

Being rooted in technology, Internet business systems and processes themselves can be leveraged in intelligent ways to help you get the biggest "bang for the buck."

When a new buyer orders a digital product from your sales website, is there a system that gets them to join your mailing list, or accept a second "upsell" offer, or join your partner program and promote your products for an affiliate commission?

Whenever you get a new customer into your business, do you have a process by which you can interact with them, find out if you delivered value, and then leverage that "delight factor" into recruiting the new buyer into helping spread word about you and your business to their contacts?

Every time a new reader signs up to your email newsletter, do you have a way to invite them to share each issue with a friend, or re-publish your content, or send a download or registration link to people they know who may find it interesting?

Setting up such processes are one-time activities that can keep your business growing exponentially, pretty much on autopilot!

These were things I learned only after many years of running my information business. By knowing the power and value of leverage, you'll gain a head start over many others who are still struggling to grow their business, and keep yours expanding by leaps and bounds while they stagnate or plateau off.

Integration

For many beginner infopreneurs (entrepreneurs who are profiting from creating information resources), the greatest emphasis and focus is on a single product. They may work hard to sell an e-book, or a DVD program, or a digital course, and direct all their marketing efforts towards that end.

But even if it works and brings in many sales, the profit potential from such an approach is severely restricted because making the first sale is always expensive. You are working to convince a prospect about your trustworthiness, creating desire for the product or service that you sell, and pushing them down the slippery slope to pulling out their credit card and paying you money for it.

That's hard work. It often takes multiple exposures over a period of time. And that costs money (or time).

For a long while, I was caught in this trap myself - before realizing what other smarter infopreneurs were doing right from the beginning... selling multiple products! By putting in the same effort as I did, they were netting far bigger profits than me. They were working smarter, not harder!

What's more, a happy buyer will readily order your other products (or even things that you recommend highly) - giving you a larger profit margin in future sales.

This is why having a "back-end" or "follow on" offer (preferably many of them) becomes critically important if you're looking to maximize your profit and the value from every new client in your business.

Integrating these multiple offers into your selling process can take some thought and careful planning. You must come up with relevant, targeted offers to make your buyers. You must try out different approaches to see which ones appeal most to your audience. And you will have to experiment with things like the intervals at which you will send out promotions for other products to your buyers, the pricing of these offers, and how you will reward loyal customers over new ones.

Integration goes far beyond just making more offers, though.

You can integrate different elements like marketing. These may be simple ideas like "auto-responder swaps," a mutual arrangement with a marketing partner where you get your marketing message included in their automated follow-up email sequence to their buyers, in exchange for you running their ad to your buyers.

Or you may come up with more elaborate arrangements like "thank you page exchanges" where you get your offer integrated into someone else's post-purchase page, where a new customer, fresh from buying something, will see your offer and possibly order it too.

Another element that you'll get enormous value from integrating into your selling is a powerful purpose. My own information business was created to meet a need. Writing is actually my hobby. My real professional calling is as a pediatric heart surgeon. I treat little children born with life-threatening heart defects, many from families that cannot afford the cost of surgery.

My Internet based information business raises funds that help sponsor their treatment. And integrating this "powerful purpose" into my business processes creates the beautiful synergy of making my customers feel good about the money they spend with my business, and giving them one more good reason to come back and buy again.

Each element layers upon another. A back-end offer made to buyers, integrated into a series of other selling processes, all powered by a purpose that appeals to your prospective buyers, can help create a finely tuned machine that pulls in more sales and profits than any of them in isolation can do.

All of this requires some strategic thinking about your business:
- Seeing how the parts fit together.
- Arranging them in a manner that is logical.
- Presenting them in an attractive fashion.
- Organizing them in way that can scale and grow with your business.

Even if it sounds difficult, it really isn't. And putting it off until later only makes you under-perform to your fullest potential by way of profits and sales maximization.

There are probably a dozen more things I wish I'd known when getting started with my online business. And five or 10 years from now, I'm sure I'll wish there were other things I'd known today. That's the nature of the beast called Internet business. It changes, evolves and morphs over time. As you gain in experience, skill and knowledge, you become aware of new things that can help you get more from everything you do.

Learning how to improve your business is a never-ending process. Be willing and ready to keep on learning, keep on testing, and keep on growing.

Hopefully the three lessons - branding, leverage and integration - will serve you well along the way.

Editors' note

Dr Mani, who's been profiled and celebrated by such luminaries as Fast Company and Seth Godin, proves that everyone - even the "big dogs" can struggle when they first start their web-based business. When he started, there was a dirth of knowledge. Today, as Dr. Mani points out, there's a sea of knowledge -- and confusion.

You need to know you can trust the experts and mentors you listen to.

Starting a business - either on the web or on Main Street, requires tools - assets. You have lots of tools (assets, skills, talents etc) at your disposal as we've discussed in other chapters. But one asset - the one Dr. Mani talks about - is that ability to take in information, and creatively apply it, leveraging not only the information you've just learned, but also integrating it with your existing base of information, and transforming that information into something even more valuable.

You - you were the secret ingredient.

Focus on being in business - not for today or to get through this economy. Focus on the long haul. Focus on being in business and conducting business on the Internet AS IF you were one of those old time Main Street merchants who had to look their customers, friends, neighbors, church congregants, in the eye every day and face whether they were doing the right thing by their customers and community each and every day.

Knowing then who you are, what you're about, and what you want to be known for then become part of your business' core values - the values you can run a business on for a lifetime. That's real branding -- not just the Nike or Microsoft kind of branding that can be bought and paid for through millions of dollars of advertising. When done right - YOU are your brand. And your reputation becomes your advertising campaign.

The risk as Dr. Mani points out, is balancing the need to be focused without being restrictive in your thought (too focused). Sound contradictory? Not at all. If you've done your homework (as we've alluded to in previous chapters) and know who you are, and what you are about (branding), what your strengths are and what your customer needs, you'll start to see a virtual mind map of opportunities - interconnected because they all serve the same customer, and they all are within the scope of your brand.

Dr. Mani's example is self-evident. As an infopreneur who's ventures fund medical miracles for those who can't afford them, Dr. Mani shows all of us that you <u>can</u> "do good" while doing good and that such "personal values" can (and should) influence the vision of our businesses.

For more information about this author, or to learn more about how to start your own web-based business, go to <u>www.mcmoodycrawford.com</u>. There you can also sign up for our newsletter and announcements about our upcoming events.

ABOUT TAHIR SHAH

Tahir Shah is an online marketer and sales training expert living in Manchester, England. Tahir owns and runs a successful offline sales training company and has earned over a million dollars online. Before turning towards Internet marketing, Tahir worked as a consultant with offline companies helping to transform them from start up enterprises into multi-million pound concerns.

11

DON'T LET WEB MONSTERS BE YOUR MASTER

by TAHIR SHAH
www.autobuildit.com

When I started out, I wish I had known that I don't NEED to know as much as I originally thought I did, in order to make a decent online income. Unfortunately, that very same thought is something that almost everyone looking at the Internet as a means of income falls foul of, and there's evidence of that everywhere you look... IF you can recognize what you're looking for.

It's the monster that Internet marketing forums reverberate with the sound of.

It's the demon thriving on the ghosts of long gone would be marketers, who's efforts in vain still haunt the Internet, whilst the demon searches to drive despair into the minds of new, eager, would-be online entrepreneurs... in the hope of sealing their fate as those gone before.

It's the stalker that once finds its target, never lets it escape from its sight.

It's the number one newbie killer: Information overload.

Yet information overload really serves a greater master.

It's the symptom, not the cause of the failure.

It's the scapegoat, not the guilty party.

It took me some time to realize this, and it's something that most people never realize until it's too late. They realize they've wasted their money, invested their time, read all about the greatest techniques, and have not got anything to show for it.

Then the questions begin to mount: So how does this happen? Where does it start? What causes it to develop? What is the real cause and most importantly how do you combat it?

It's an alien environment

Let's look at the scenario of an alien in human form landing on Earth from another planet and wanting to learn about humans playing sport. The research begins:
- What is sport?
- What sports are there?
- What are their rules?
- How are they played?

So our human look-alike alien, in order to learn about sports, starts learning about football (soccer for those of you on the other side of the pond), cricket, boxing, fencing, gymnastics, badminton, squash… you get the point.

Will any of that make the alien become a great tennis player? A great sweeper? A great boxer? A great fencer? A great gymnast?

The answer to that is "No". Now, the alien might be a great boxer… might be a great fencer… might be a great gymnast… or great at something else, but only if he or she (or it?) tried out the sports and got involved, would he, she (or it) find out. On the other hand the alien might be an absolute failure at the sports, but would certainly learn more through practicing a particular sport, rather than just reading about it.

But what does the alien do? Thinks to his or herself "I don't know about enough about sports yet… there are many other sports I've not learned about, how they're played, and the rules governing them."

In just the same way, so it is with those entering the online world of business.

108 million answers to one question

"What is Internet marketing?" That, entered as a search term in Google, brings around 108 million-search results. So it is no surprise how someone starting an Internet marking business finds his or herself in a state of information overload.

It is just like the analogy of an alien visitor from another planet trying to learn about sports on Earth, because this concept of marketing on the Internet is ALIEN to most anyone who wants to do it. They start from the proverbial square one.

And soon enough they start asking all of the usual questions: What is html? What is ftp? What is a squeeze page? What is email marketing? What are auto responders? What is SEO? What is social media marketing? What is... ? And the list goes on and on. These are all legitimate questions, ones that even the Internet gurus of today asked at one time, even though they may not admit it now.

However, instead of just getting a domain name, buying some hosting, and using an ftp program to get their first page online, they feel they don't know enough yet... so they continue to learn more... and learn more... and learn even more.

Then finally, when, or even if they ever do try and get their page online, it looks so shoddy, because they're not a designer and not a programmer. So they go back to learning – buying books, magazines, subscribing to sites, listening to webinars and buying bright shiny objects -- thinking that will provide the answers for poor conversions, no traffic, and no business.

They are doing something. It feels SAFER than continuing to try doing something online.

This is something that I learned very early on: You don't need to be an Internet marketing expert to make money online. There are many Internet marketing experts filling the forums who have never earned a bean. Conversely, there are many people, just like me, who know just enough to get by, but end up making fortunes, because they know where to focus their efforts.

Five key components to success

To be successful online, there are ONLY five key components that you really need to focus on.

    1.   Have a product or service to sell.

2. Brand yourself as an expert (and that doesn't mean necessarily an Internet marketing expert).
3. Find JV partners or affiliates or another method to drive traffic to your website and promote your products.
4. Build a mailing list.
5. Know how to sell your product online through proven online sales principles.

That's it. The rest is just sugar coating, and those that are successful online focus on those activities whilst the rest of the world chases secret strategy after secret strategy and pay through the nose for the privilege of so. Yet they fail to focus their efforts on what they should be doing... the five points mentioned above.

So they stay sitting in the classroom learning more, and suffering from the inevitable information overload.

Successful webpreneurs outsource

Those who are making money online and are successful, can afford to pay others so that technology doesn't get in their way of progress and doesn't paralyze them from moving ahead swiftly with their plans. They outsource, they pay programmers and designers to do things for them that they know they can't do.

Your average marketer however tries to do everything DIY and fails miserably.

Not being able to master technology is the key killer - NOT the information overload – of average marketers. You see most marketers aren't trained programmers or designers, and aside from those who've got the bucks to hire their own, most people struggle when it comes to technology and how to get their websites to do what they **need** them to do.

If you're skilled in those areas already, to a point where you could do them professionally for others, then, and only then should you do them for yourself. Otherwise you run the risk of what you're creating being seen for what it is: amateurish.

However here's where the problem really lies. Most people aren't professional designers and programmers. Professional designers usually aren't also professional programmers, and vice-versa; And often they know less about marketing than professional marketers who don't have those skills, but who do nothing but study marketing.

So on the one hand, you have true marketing experts who've spent too long sitting in the classroom and far too long for them NOT to be able to use what they've learned to make them an online income. Why? Simply because they don't know how to transform their visions into professional looking online realities... and on the other hand, you have professional programmers and designers who don't know enough about Internet marketing and how much more they could do if they did.

You see, good programming and good design take a lot of time. A LOT of time.

So for marketers, who won't or don't employ professional designers or programmers to do the work that they can't, they often resort to a halfway house solution: Buy readymade templates which they can simply alter the text on. And that usually means single paged websites, or mini-site templates that they're restricted with, because they can't alter the look and feel of that page without messing up, because of the CSS style sheets that restrict their options and their limited skills.

And believe me when I say: all experienced marketers have faced exactly the same problems too.

These experienced marketers are not better at doing these things, but they have people who can do what they want done.

Let me put it this way. I hate anything technical. And I mean *hate anything* technical. It takes me hours to do the same thing, my designer or programmers could do in a matter of a few seconds or minutes, and I've experienced that scenario many times.

Why?

First: I'd have to learn how to do it.

Second: I inevitably end up breaking something else whilst trying to implement the solution I'm trying to implement. If I find a piece of JavaScript that I want to add to a page, and it conflicts with another script that's already on there... how would I fix it? The answer is... I haven't got the foggiest idea. By the way, if you don't know what JavaScript is, believe me, other than knowing it's a piece of code that magically performs some kind of cool function, neither do I.

And I don't ever want to know those things. I'd hate having to learn how to do it. I don't even know how to set up a blog. I know basic html, and I mean basic; how to create links and add them to payment buttons and how to create headlines – that kind of stuff. And I hate having to do any of that too. It's time consuming and laborious and I often still get things wrong. I'm just not technical at all when it comes to a lot of this stuff, and believe it or not, neither are many of the really successful marketers online.

They know what they need to know, and not more. Then they leverage the expertise of those who know what they don't, and get them to do what they can't do.

In the meantime, the best Internet marketers focus their energies on improving five things; they make sure they're great at them. What are these things? You guessed... the same skills I mentioned before:
1. Creating/sourcing products or services to sell.
2. Branding themselves as an expert.
3. Finding JV partners/affiliates or other methods to drive traffic to their offerings.
4. Building their mailing lists.
5. Improving their sales and conversions.

They don't sit around learning every new strategy their email inbox throws at them. Instead they make sure that they're getting what they do know in an online format that generates them further sales and profits.

Now remember, all Internet marketing superstars started out just like you: me included. I didn't enter the online arena with a programming team. I didn't have a design team waiting to act on my every instruction. I had the same learning curve, the same information overload process. But I also had the "Eureka!" moment, realizing that I could not afford to stay "sitting in the classroom," or in learning mode. I realized I was suffering information overload because I didn't have the technical skills to do what I needed to get done.

So I started putting up amateur looking pages that performed the basic function of selling, building a mailing list, and getting my name out there. And I got mediocre results and sales as a result of that.

Competition has changed

However, that was quite a few years ago in a much more forgiving time. People seemed more interested in what you had to say at that time. There was far less competition in people's email inboxes, and there weren't several launches a day being promoted by thousands of affiliates hitting everyone's email inbox, as there are now.

Nowadays, to be successful, you can't afford to have an amateur look if you want to get ahead online. Today, to be able to compete with the top marketers, you have to be able to do all the things that they are able to do with the help of designers and programmers. You have to be able to use video marketing, produce timed "Buy Now" buttons that magically appear, create page redirects, and all of the other things that are working for marketers who are making the big bucks.

So, if you don't have the time to learn them, what do you do?

People still try to take the easy no-cost route and put their sales videos up on YouTube and embed them from their sites, but that might be going against YouTube's "terms of service," and looks amateur too.

As technology advances, you have to keep up. If you're like me and not technical, how do you do that? That's the real major problem for most people and that's the problem that holds a lot people back from.

Now fortunately I have a programming team. I have a design team. And so do many of the top successful marketers or have people who they use often and regularly.

However a problem still arises. When my programmers are not around and I need something technical doing, I am stuck. When my designers are not around and I need something designing, I'm stuck. And so is any other marketer, and so will you be even when you have a programming or design team of your own.

Now I mention these things to let you know that you're not alone in things that hold you back, and that those very same things hold even successful marketers back, when they do not have immediate access to them.

And programmers and designers can cost a pretty penny, which is why for many people until they are earning money; it's just not a viable option.

So here in 2011 I found myself asking a few simple questions.

"Despite having a programming and design team... why am I still struggling when they're not around?"

And the answer is the same for me, today, as it always has been. And it will be the same 10 years from now: I hate doing anything technical because it takes me ages to do it, so I often end up NOT doing it.

Being aware of that, made me do as many of those things myself when I could and knew how to. Now, when it comes to those tasks, I rely much on my guys and gals to do it for me. And so will you, once you have them. But that's as much about necessity, as it is about laziness.

What lesson have I learned?

I recognize this now. So should you. Because here is the real reason that separates those who are successful online from those who are not:

A person's ability to become successful online is <u>directly</u> <u>proportional</u> to how easily he or she can conquer the technological challenges that stop them from making the progress they need to make.
What I've just told you is so important for your online success that you need to write that down somewhere. Memorize it. Don't ever forget it.
If you're not making headway online, the major factor stopping you is more than likely some technological challenge.

Quite simply, this realization took advantage of my resources. This year, I got my programmers started on creating a tool, which will allow me to do anything I want to do easily and simply. Granted, this is more than a beginning Internet marketer can do, but it does demonstrate what can be a reality if you apply the five principles described previously in this chapter.

Knowledge has never been the problem for most marketers. It's the technology that has slowed them down from doing what they need to do. That coupled with lack of focus.

So focus on the five key elements I've mentioned already, and start working on creating your online presence that allows you to achieve those things. That's the true route to success. Don't just read e-book after e-book or falling for push button solutions that don't work.

And if you find a tool that allows you to conquer the technology that's so far held you back? You don't have to be Einstein to know that you need to at least take a look it, and if you can see it does everything you want to do but you can't do on your own... then quite simply... use it.

Editors' note
Tahir Shah provides great advice to help stave off the newbie Internet Marketer assassin: Information Overload.

First - determine if you really do want to make a living online. This relates back to numerous comments throughout this book regarding understanding who you are, your goals, etc.

Second - yes, you are going to need to do some research. But don't let yourself get caught up in "analysis paralysis." Learn very quickly what tasks or items are things that you have to do because you are the value add to the offering. And while you might need to understand basic steps or processes, you don't need to become a programmer, designer, etc. There are plenty of affordable freelancers available to help you with various functional areas.

Third - understand the difference between being an expert and making yourself a "self appointed expert." You do need to be an expert - at your business, at your core business, at what you do. But don't follow, as Tahir points out, simply take on a title of being an expert in just any topic or anything. Not representing yourself authentically does you and your potential customers a disservice: not only are you not communicating your real expertise, but you are also damaging the trust with your target audience.

Building a business is a bit like remodeling a house. With the advent of D-I-Y, people all over the world are now trying to take the process of remodeling their homes into their own hands -- to mixed results. The difference between remodeling a home and building a business is that when you are remodeling a home, the major systems (electrical, plumbing, HVAC, etc) are all in place (usually). When you build a new home, however, none of these systems are in place: and either you, or someone you hire (a licensed plumber, electrician, contractor) does it.

The dynamic between the DIY parts of anyone (the appeal of pulling yourself up by your own bootstraps and accomplishing anything you set your mind to) is often in conflict with the vital need of understanding that some things are just best left to professionals who specialize in the topic. When we're talking about DIY heart surgery (or not) the decision is easy: get the surgeon. But when we are talking about things like business.... sometimes the lines become more blurred. That the Internet has become about "instant everything" and is certainly far easier, faster and less expensive to start a business on than starting a physical storefront doesn't help. New webpreneurs are often lulled by the relative "ease" of it all, and lead into a false sense of ability to "do it all themselves."

So focus on what you know: you know your vision of your business. And if you don't have a vision, slow down and do more research so you can focus and find your vision. You can't outsource the leadership of your business. You are the leadership.

Perhaps the most profound, but unspoken lesson from Tahir is: you <u>can</u> have it all. You can set a dream and going about making that dream come true. But you can't do it all (as in doing everything in your business, start up through life cycle management), and still <u>have</u> it all. Invariably, something, like your health, family situation, or business process, will *crack.*

For more information about this author, or to learn more about how to start your own web-based business, go to www.mcmoodycrawford.com. There you can also sign up for our newsletter and announcements about our upcoming events.

12

IN SUMMARY: DEVELOPING YOUR OWN GPS SYSTEM

by DRs CHRISTINA McCALE and RICHARD D. MOODY
www.mcmoodycrawford.com

The picture of the web industry, or Internet Marketing (IM) as some of the authors call it, is not a pretty one. It's exciting – full of change and advancement. But it's also a challenging market for even the most seasoned of pros as some of our author experts have shared.

While the image of being inundated by marketing and information, can be intimidating, there are processes and tips the authors have all shared that will help you on your path.

These stories woven throughout the book can provide insight and inspiration to so many who have found themselves trapped in the tectonic shifts in our economy and society. By learning from these experts, you can begin to work the discovery process, learning more about who you are and what skills you possess that will serve you well in a web-based business.

Much of what we know or believe about doing business on the web has been warped by urban legend and exaggeration. While much about the Internet is, indeed, instant, building a business and ensuring its success and long-term viability is not.

All businesses – both on and offline - require effort, planning, processes, and TIME. Which brings us to our first major category of advice: Business Practices.

Business Practices

It's probably no accident or coincidence that the majority (52%) of unaided, unprompted advice had something to do with the actual establishment and growth of a business.

While this is certainly also shaped by the scope of the book as laid out by the authors, it also speaks to an important element: getting off on the right foot is important.

Doing so requires understanding and applying the tips and advice threaded throughout the book, but all circulate around one essential process: taking the time to do the research, focus your efforts on a given market that could benefit from your unique skills, assets and abilities. Learn as much as you about your market, your potential customers, and their needs.

Get a sense of the competitive market space and the environmental factors affecting your market. Such planning and understanding then leads to establishing goals both for your personal and professional life.

If you aren't sure what you want from your business, if you can't explain what it is you want to do, how you want your business to be perceived, how much revenue you realistically need…. Then keep searching for your answers.

You can still start taking baby steps while you're learning. But keep working at it. You are the secret ingredient to your company's future. You are the keeper of the vision; the holder of the company's values – even if your company is a "company" of one.

You are the one who determines what your firm will be about. While you can keep bringing that vision into sharper focus – you must be actively working towards getting that focus.

Through that focusing process, you'll find that many activities, time suckers, and sales pitches for the latest and greatest product become extraneous – totally unnecessary -- because they don't do anything to support your main goal of creating a successful business.

Given the group of entrepreneurs involved in this book, it's feasible that their advice to future webpreneurs to develop solid business fundamentals and foundation comes from their own previous life and/or career experiences. The large majority of these authors had previous experiences in business or organizational life prior to building a web based business.

So the question remains – where does one get this experience that many of our expert authors had and were able to capitalize on? Is working in the offline environment for someone else really needed to be successful? Does formalized education matter? These questions were not part of the scope of the study, however it may not be too big of a leap to presume that the authors' translatable skills from previous educational and professional experiences did inform their venture into web-based businesses.

Therefore it might benefit newcomers who have little to no business acumen to spend time learning the principles of business.

Also, perhaps shaped by the topic of the book, was the notably missing absence of other fundamentals of starting a business such as the legal aspects, operations, and – while some was discussed – finance.

Are these the areas that are simply "less glamorous" than such topics as marketing, strategy and management? Understanding how these topics are perceived in relative importance in the eyes of the webpreneur will be further studied.

Marketing

Planning and getting established can only get you so far. So often webpreneurs spend so much time, money and effort building their product, business, website (or book) that by the time it's ready to launch, they're out of the vital resources needed to take their business to the next phase: Actually marketing it. "If you build it, [they] will come" might work for Kevin Costner in the cornfields of Iowa –but it's not a sound business strategy.

The advice in this section was only 17% of all the tips and advice provided. But 100% of the advice hinged on shoestring, low budget approaches that virtually any webpreneur could implement.

Further, through the authors' stories and examples we see that at the end of the day, for all the high-tech solutions on the web today, people still like doing business with people. So implementing "old economy" business activities in "new economy ways" would be wise for any entrepreneur to consider.

So for example:

Old Economy Marketing Activities	New Economy Marketing Equivalents
Word of Mouth	Social Media, conversing on blog platforms, forums
Attending local Chamber meetings	Attend "live" in person events or trainings focused on web marketing.
Direct Mail	Email marketing
Phone Book Directory Advertising	Directory/location based listings such as on Google Places
Coupon Mailers or weekly store circulars	Mass group purchasing programs, such as Groupon
Sales people "telling" your customers about their challenges and how your business can help them	More information based sales: providing information through a variety of article directories, offering webinars, special reports to educate your customer
Creating "multiple locations" convenient located for your customers	Using various services such as YouTube, Twitter, and Facebook as "outposts" for your main website.
Putting up a website and expecting customers to come to you	Going to your customer – making your site and its message convenient and comprehendible in a variety of situations, to include mobile.

Marketing is the simple act of making your message (whether about your product, company or person) made known; great marketing makes sales easier.

But in a world where acronyms and technology are changing faster than the latest "Real Housewives" scandal, perhaps it's helpful to consistently align the "old means" of marketing and translating them into what our new technology allows us to do – often for far less money, far more focused, and far faster than ever before.

It's easy to get lost in the malaise of the technology – particularly for new webpreneurs who may not particularly have a strong background in web-based technologies. So consider going back to that purest version of the business exchange: how do they know you exist? What is it you are offering for sale? What makes you different? If you were doing business in your hometown on Main Street – how would people get information about you? Now, find out what that manner – or marketing vehicle – is being reinvented into in the New Economy.

For all of its importance, the discussion of marketing in the role of a new business was slightly less than might typically be expected. Further, the absence of discussion regarding traditional media or marketing efforts, holistic, integrated marketing communications, pricing, and other common marketing core subject areas has ensured this will be an ongoing topic of inquiry.

Operations

Getting your business up and running is one thing. Keeping it running is another. The authors focused on key areas for new web marketers not to forget: Data backup, Goal Setting, Daily Planning, and working with other firms in partnership or outsourcing situations. Each topic important, but tending to be quite tactical in nature.

Each of these topics could indeed probably be topics of entire books themselves. But we find it curious that more focus was not placed on this area. This may be a distinction between Internet Marketing and traditional businesses that spend significant time and effort on the "back end" of the business before engaging the customer. It is a topic we will pursue in further research.

Keeping your sanity

As with any research, there is always a surprise element to the data. This was ours. Our partner Willie Crawford is the evangelist here: You are your own secret ingredient. You are your own super hero. Therefore, YOU must protect YOU. Hence, the topic of keeping your sanity as a webpreneur.

Perhaps by the sheer, isolated nature of web-based businesses, there comes a growth or emphasis on the individual, even more so than their off-line entrepreneurial counterparts. Because it is a solo-act, because of the technology, and because so much can be outsourced to others, being a webpreneur is, to use an old phrase, "All About You:" not only is it about your business idea, but it is about YOU, the brand; it's about you, your business strengths, your goals, your idea of what a perfect work-life balance looks like. The business, if you are wise, is built to suit your needs as a human being, rather than to suit the conventional expectation of what society deems is "success."

Many of the authors discussed the perils of information overload, the compelling and conflicting needs to be constantly investing in yourself and your knowledge but yet maintaining balance. However, as the discussions show, the investment in one's self as a webpreneur then becomes the connective tissue between your business life and your plan for your life. Most entrepreneurs barely adequately plan their businesses; how many create equally meaningful plans for what they want their lives to look like? How many will then integrate the two to see how the two plans not only can, but must, work together? This, too, is an area of untapped potential for exploration and comparison with traditional, offline entrepreneurs.

But just as it was discussed in the Business Practices segment, planning and goal setting is vital to continuously fostering growth, change and success. The same could be said of your own Life Plan. By creating a map that includes a plan for both your personal and professional lives, you can attain that degree of balance, integration and holistic branding that many of the authors referenced.

ABOUT OUR EDITORS

Dr. Christina McCale

Prior to getting her doctorate in Marketing, Chris worked for 17+ years in corporate America at AT&T, US West, Qwest, and American Red Cross). As part of her marketing responsibilities, Chris ran multi-state, multi-million dollar research projects that directly impacted the strategic planning and product development for the firms she worked for.

In addition to her marketing and management instructional duties at the university level at such schools as Regis University, Denver, The Metropolitan State College of Denver, and University of Phoenix, for the last 10 years, she has also been one of the key researchers auditing what universities are doing (or *not doing*) to prepare undergraduates for real careers after college; and as a result, has been named one of the most prolific writers/researchers in marketing education in the last 10 years by the Journal of Marketing Education. Previous to her marketing career, Chris was in broadcast journalism.

In addition to her doctorate, Chris has her bachelor's in journalism and master's in organizational leadership from Gonzaga University, as well as advanced graduate studies in marketing at the University of Colorado – Denver.

Dr. Richard D. Moody.

As a political reporter, Dick honed his interviewing and editing skills covering an array of policy issues, ranging from covering local school board meetings for a weekly newspaper to interviewing presidents and presidential candidates for a metropolitan daily.

Dick later worked in for profit and non-profit in the education area, including eight years with Apple's education division, Houghton Mifflin's assessment group, and the non-profit national Association of Educational Service Agencies and Northwest Evaluation Association. He has his doctorate in education leadership from Seattle University, master's in organizational leadership from Gonzaga University, and bachelor's in journalism from Central Washington University. He is also affiliate faculty at Regis University's School of Education.

·

11727055R0009

Made in the USA
Lexington, KY
26 October 2011